CAMBRIDGE SCHOOL

Shakespeare

The Comedy of Errors

Edited by Richard Andrews

Series Editor: Rex Gibson
Director, Shakespeare and Schools Project

CAMBRIDGE
UNIVERSITY PRESS

CAMBRIDGE UNIVERSITY PRESS
Cambridge, New York, Melbourne, Madrid, Cape Town, Singapore, São Paulo

Cambridge University Press
The Edinburgh Building, Cambridge CB2 2RU, UK

www.cambridge.org
Information on this title: www.cambridge.org/9780521395755

First published 1992
Reprinted with amendments 1993
7th printing 2006

Printed in the United Kingdom at the University Press, Cambridge

A catalogue record for this publication is available from the British Library

ISBN-13 978-0-521-39575-5 paperback
ISBN-10 0-521-39575-5 paperback

Designed by Richard Morris
Illustration by Jones and Sewell Associates
Picture research by Callie Kendall

The extract from 'Sir Henry Morgan's Song' by Edwin Morgon on p. 16 is
reproduced by from *Collected Poems* by permission of Carcanet Press Limited.

Thanks are due to the following for permission to reproduce photographs:

p. 10, Boydell Collection in Forest Collection, p. 229, Birmingham Shakespeare Library,
Birmingham Library Services; pp. 18, 115*l*, Joe Cocks Studio; pp. 22, 96, Clive Barda; p. 24,
The Master and Fellows, Magdalene College, Cambridge; p. 28, © Desmond Tripp/
Birmingham Shakespeare Library ref. C270, Birmingham Library Services; p. 32, Zentral-
biblothek, Zurich; p. 38, Forest Collection, p. 335, Birmingham Shakespeare Library,
Birmingham Library Services; p. 46*t*, Birmingham Shakespeare Library ref. s.601.14, Birming-
ham Library Services; p. 46*b*, © Alan Daiches/Birmingham Shakespeare Library ref. 601.14,
Birmingham Library Services; p. 54, Forrest Collection, Birmingham Shakespeare Library,
Birmingham Library Services; p. 62, Shakespeare Centre Library, Stratford-upon-Avon; p. 74,
Forrest Collection, p. 267, Birmingham Shakespeare Library, Birmingham Library Services;
pp. 80, 87, © Alastair Muir; Birmingham Library Services; p. 113, By gracious permission of
the Masters of the Bench of the Honourable Society of Gray's Inn; pp. 121, 123, Shakespeare
Centre Library, Stratford-upon-Avon.

Contents

Cambridge School Shakespeare

This edition of *The Comedy of Errors* is part of the *Cambridge School Shakespeare* series. Like every other play in the series, it has been specially prepared to help all students in schools and colleges.

This *The Comedy of Errors* aims to be different from other editions of the play. It invites you to bring the play to life in your classroom, hall or drama studio through enjoyable activities that will increase your understanding. Actors have created their different interpretations of the play over the centuries. Similarly, you are encouraged to make up your own mind about *The Comedy of Errors*, rather than having someone else's interpretation handed down to you.

Cambridge School Shakespeare does not offer you a cut-down or simplified version of the play. This is Shakespeare's language, filled with imaginative possibilities. You will find on every left-hand page: a summary of the action, an explanation of unfamiliar words, a choice of activities on Shakespeare's language, characters and stories.

Between each act and in the pages at the end of the play, you will find notes, illustrations and activities. These will help to increase your understanding of the whole play.

There are a large number of activities to give you the widest choice to suit your own particular needs. Please don't think you have to do every one. Choose the activities that will help you most.

This edition will be of value to you whether you are studying for an examination, reading for pleasure, or thinking of putting on the play to entertain others. You can work on the activities on your own or in groups. Many of the activities suggest a particular group size, but don't be afraid to make up larger or smaller groups to suit your own purposes.

Although you are invited to treat *The Comedy of Errors* as a play, you don't need special dramatic or theatrical skills to do the activities. By choosing your activities, and by exploring and experimenting, you can make your own interpretations of Shakespeare's language, characters and stories. Whatever you do, remember that Shakespeare wrote his plays to be acted, watched and enjoyed.

Rex Gibson

This edition of *The Comedy of Errors* uses the text of the play established by T. S. Dorsch in *The New Cambridge Shakespeare*.

List of characters

SOLINUS	Duke of Ephesus
EGEON	a merchant of Syracuse, and Aemilia's husband
AEMILIA	Abbess at Ephesus, and Egeon's wife
ANTIPHOLUS of Syracuse	twin son of Aemilia and Egeon
ANTIPHOLUS of Ephesus	twin son of Aemilia and Egeon
ADRIANA	wife of Antipholus of Ephesus
LUCIANA	Adriana's sister
DROMIO of Syracuse	twin slave of the Antipholuses
DROMIO of Ephesus	twin slave of the Antipholuses
LUCE (or NELL)	Adriana's kitchen-maid
A COURTESAN	
BALTHASAR	a merchant
ANGELO	a goldsmith
FIRST MERCHANT	
SECOND MERCHANT	
DR PINCH	a schoolmaster/conjurer
AN OFFICER	
A JAILER	
A MESSENGER	
OFFICERS, HEADSMAN, ATTENDANTS	

All the action takes place in the town of Ephesus in a single day.

Egeon asks for the death sentence to put an end to his misery. The Duke explains that Egeon will die because of the trade war between Ephesus and Syracuse. Egeon's only hope of avoiding death is by ransom.

1 What has just happened? (in groups of two, three or four)

Based on the dialogue opposite, enact (and possibly write the script of) what might have come immediately before the opening lines. You may want to use just two characters – Egeon and Solinus – or give lines to the jailer and/or other attendants who can act as witnesses or chorus.

2 Follow the action

Trace the course of Egeon's story (lines 36–139) on a copy of this map.

partial to inclined to	**seditious** rebellious, subversive
guilders money	**synods** councils or assemblies
bloods lives	**traffic** business
intestine jars deadly quarrels	**dispose** disposal

The Comedy of Errors

ACT I   SCENE I
Ephesus   The market-place

Enter SOLINUS, *the Duke of Ephesus, with* EGEON, *the merchant of Syracuse,* JAILER *and other attendants*

EGEON Proceed, Solinus, to procure my fall,
      And by the doom of death end woes and all.
DUKE Merchant of Syracusa, plead no more.
      I am not partial to infringe our laws.
      The enmity and discord which of late   5
      Sprung from the rancorous outrage of your Duke
      To merchants, our well-dealing countrymen,
      Who, wanting guilders to redeem their lives,
      Have sealed his rigorous statutes with their bloods,
      Excludes all pity from our threatening looks.   10
      For since the mortal and intestine jars
      'Twixt thy seditious countrymen and us
      It hath in solemn synods been decreed
      Both by the Syracusians and ourselves
      To admit no traffic to our adverse towns.   15
      Nay, more: if any born at Ephesus
      Be seen at Syracusian marts and fairs;
      Again, if any Syracusian born
      Come to the bay of Ephesus, he dies,
      His goods confiscate to the Duke's dispose,   20
      Unless a thousand marks be levièd
      To quit the penalty and to ransom him.

Egeon cannot raise the money to free himself. At the Duke's command,
he begins to tell the story of his twin sons and their twin servants.

1 Telling the story

Egeon relates the story of his unlucky life in lines 36–139. There are
various ways to re-tell this story. Choose one of the following ways (or
another not suggested here) to re-tell it to a particular audience (e.g.
young children, teenagers, university professors, factory workers):

- in comic strip (with or without the text)
- in mime (with or without narrator)
- in prose, as an autobiographical story
- briefly, in twenty-five rather than 100 lines; then in ten lines;
  then one!
- as a cross-examination
- from someone else's point of view
- using several characters to tell the story.

2 On-stage reactions (in groups of four to six)

Talk together about producing the scene on stage. The long story that
Egeon tells presents you with a problem: what is everyone going to do
while Egeon tells his story? Choose one of these ways of presenting
his story:

- as a dream sequence or flashback
- using the attendants as 'chess pieces' to depict the story
- using props, like photographs of his family taken from his wallet
- a map of the eastern Mediterranean Sea and a pointer
- using a blackboard and chalk.

Decide who Egeon's audience is going to be. Then, using any of the
ideas suggested here or in 'Telling the story' (above), act out Egeon's
story.

---

substance worth
wrought by nature brought about
  naturally, through his love for his
  son

hap luck
factor agent
at random without care
mean poor

Thy substance, valued at the highest rate,
Cannot amount unto a hundred marks;
Therefore by law thou art condemned to die.   25
EGEON Yet this my comfort: when your words are done,
My woes end likewise with the evening sun.
DUKE Well, Syracusian, say in brief the cause
Why thou departed'st from thy native home,
And for what cause thou cam'st to Ephesus.   30
EGEON A heavier task could not have been imposed
Than I to speak my griefs unspeakable.
Yet, that the world may witness that my end
Was wrought by nature, not by vile offence,
I'll utter what my sorrow gives me leave.   35
In Syracusa was I born, and wed
Unto a woman happy but for me,
And by me, had not our hap been bad.
With her I lived in joy, our wealth increased
By prosperous voyages I often made   40
To Epidamnum, till my factor's death,
And the great care of goods at random left,
Drew me from kind embracements of my spouse,
From whom my absence was not six months old
Before herself (almost at fainting under   45
The pleasing punishment that women bear)
Had made provision for her following me,
And soon and safe arrivèd where I was.
There had she not been long but she became
A joyful mother of two goodly sons;   50
And, which was strange, the one so like the other
As could not be distinguished but by names.
That very hour, and in the self-same inn,
A mean woman was deliverèd
Of such a burden male, twins both alike.   55
Those, for their parents were exceeding poor,
I bought, and brought up to attend my sons.

5

Egeon tells how the boat carrying his family was hit by a storm. He and his wife try to save the twin children and their twin servants.

---

1 Share out the speech! (in groups of four or six)

Share lines 31–95 between the members of your group. You could take turns reading, a line at a time, or only up to a punctuation mark. Or use any other ways of sharing that you think are appropriate to the speech. Once you have tried it in one way, try it in another way. Discuss which version you think works best.

Perform – or record – your speech together for the rest of the class. You can use this approach with other long speeches from the play.

2 Draw the shipwreck

Sketch the situation described by Egeon when he and his family use a mast to save themselves from the shipwreck. Include each of the characters clinging to the mast, and name them.

Compare your sketch with others, and refer back to the script to check your accuracy. If you first work in groups of four to act out lines 78–87, you'll find it helpful.

3 Family tree

Draw a family tree to show the relationships in the play so far. Compare your version with others to see if you agree. You can add to this as the play progresses.

---

motions entreaties
league 3½ miles
deep the sea
doubtful warrant frightening
  assurance
plainings wailings

delays delays from death
vapours mists
by that went before from what has
  gone before i.e. you can predict
  what happened next

My wife, not meanly proud of two such boys,
Made daily motions for our home return.
Unwilling I agreed. Alas, too soon   60
We came aboard.
A league from Epidamnum had we sailed
Before the always-wind-obeying deep
Gave any tragic instance of our harm.
But longer did we not retain much hope,   65
For what obscurèd light the heavens did grant
Did but convey unto our fearful minds
A doubtful warrant of immediate death,
Which though myself would gladly have embraced,
Yet the incessant weepings of my wife,   70
Weeping before for what she saw must come,
And piteous plainings of the pretty babes,
That mourned for fashion, ignorant what to fear,
Forced me to seek delays for them and me.
And this it was (for other means was none):   75
The sailors sought for safety by our boat,
And left the ship, then sinking-ripe, to us.
My wife, more careful for the latter-born,
Had fastened him unto a small spare mast
Such as seafaring men provide for storms.   80
To him one of the other twins was bound,
Whilst I had been like heedful of the other.
The children thus disposed, my wife and I,
Fixing our eyes on whom our care was fixed,
Fastened ourselves at either end the mast,   85
And floating straight, obedient to the stream,
Was carried towards Corinth, as we thought.
At length the sun, gazing upon the earth,
Dispersed those vapours that offended us,
And by the benefit of his wished light   90
The seas waxed calm, and we discoverèd
Two ships from far, making amain to us:
Of Corinth that, of Epidaurus this.
But ere they came – O, let me say no more.
Gather the sequel by that went before.   95

7

*Egeon tells how he and his wife were separated in the shipwreck, each with
two children. Many years later, Egeon's son resolves to find his twin brother.*

---

1 'We may pity, though not pardon thee'
(in groups of three or four)

Improvise short scenes to show the difference between pitying and
pardoning. Think of how many different contexts might fit this
contrast. Use the actual phrase in your scenes if you wish.

2 Similar stories (in pairs)

List parallel situations in which there is survival after a shipwreck
and/or someone is being sentenced to death unless certain demands
are met. Choose one of these situations and work it out in more detail.

You might like to take this further, and think of a parallel setting for
the whole play. Find costumes to suit your vision of the setting, and
act out parts of the play in pairs, using the language of Shakespeare
(see page 116).

3 All together! (whole class)

The class divides into two halves, facing each other. One half reads
Egeon's lines and the other half those of Solinus. Accompany your
words with appropriate gestures where possible.

---

worthily termed rightly called
unjust divorce unfair break-up
hap chance

reft . . . of taken from
dilate at full tell the whole story
hazarded risked

DUKE Nay, forward, old man; do not break off so,
      For we may pity, though not pardon thee.
EGEON O, had the gods done so, I had not now
      Worthily termed them merciless to us;
      For ere the ships could meet by twice five leagues   100
      We were encountered by a mighty rock,
      Which being violently borne upon,
      Our helpful ship was splitted in the midst;
      So that in this unjust divorce of us
      Fortune had left to both of us alike   105
      What to delight in, what to sorrow for.
      Her part, poor soul, seeming as burdenèd
      With lesser weight but not with lesser woe,
      Was carried with more speed before the wind,
      And in our sight they three were taken up   110
      By fishermen of Corinth, as we thought.
      At length another ship had seized on us,
      And, knowing whom it was their hap to save,
      Gave healthful welcome to their shipwracked guests,
      And would have reft the fishers of their prey   115
      Had not their bark been very slow of sail;
      And therefore homeward did they bend their course.
      Thus have you heard me severed from my bliss,
      That by misfortunes was my life prolonged
      To tell sad stories of my own mishaps.   120
DUKE And for the sake of them thou sorrow'st for,
      Do me the favour to dilate at full
      What have befall'n of them and thee till now.
EGEON My youngest boy, and yet my eldest care,
      At eighteen years became inquisitive   125
      After his brother, and importuned me
      That his attendant, so his case was like,
      Reft of his brother, but retained his name,
      Might bear him company in the quest of him;
      Whom whilst I laboured of a love to see,   130
      I hazarded the loss of whom I loved.

Egeon's travels in search of his sons have brought him to Ephesus. The Duke cannot legally change the death sentence, but gives Egeon one day to try to raise the thousand marks' ransom.

1 Find the moment in the play

Identify the characters in this 1796 engraving. Look back over lines 3–139 and choose the ones that you think best fit the illustration.

2 What next?

Predict what will happen in the rest of the play after this opening scene. You have two main pieces of evidence as the basis for your prediction: the title of the play and the nature of this first scene.

Write down your predictions, and then compare notes with a friend. Discuss your predictions with the rest of the class.

---

loath to leave . . . or any place unwilling to leave any place unexplored
warrant prove
disannul cancel

sue as advocate argue as a lawyer
limit allow
wend go
procrastinate postpone

Five summers have I spent in farthest Greece,
Roaming clean through the bounds of Asia,
And coasting homeward came to Ephesus,
Hopeless to find, yet loath to leave unsought   135
Or that or any place that harbours men.
But here must end the story of my life,
And happy were I in my timely death
Could all my travels warrant me they live.

DUKE Hapless Egeon, whom the fates have marked   140
To bear the extremity of dire mishap!
Now trust me, were it not against our laws,
Against my crown, my oath, my dignity,
Which princes, would they, may not disannul,
My soul should sue as advocate for thee.   145
But though thou art adjudgèd to the death,
And passèd sentence may not be recalled
But to our honour's great disparagement,
Yet will I favour thee in what I can.
Therefore, merchant, I'll limit thee this day   150
To seek thy health by beneficial help.
Try all the friends thou hast in Ephesus;
Beg thou or borrow to make up the sum,
And live. If no, then thou art doomed to die.
Jailer, take him to thy custody.   155

JAILER I will, my lord.

EGEON Hopeless and helpless doth Egeon wend,
But to procrastinate his lifeless end.

Exeunt

Looking back at Scene 1

1 A different beginning

The 1976 Royal Shakespeare Company production of *The Comedy of Errors* began differently from our script (lines 1–25). Identify the differences, and give possible reasons for the changes. This extract, and the song on the opposite page, are from the promptbook for the RSC production:

Enter SOLINUS, *Duke of Ephesus, and* EGEON *the merchant of Syracuse, and* GAOLER

DUKE   I am not partial to infringe our laws.
            And since the mortal and intestine jars
            'Twixt Syracusians and ourselves,
            It hath in solemn synods been decreed
            Both by the Syracusians and ourselves
            To admit no traffic to our adverse towns.
            Nay, more:
            If any born at Ephesus be seen
            At any Syracusian marts and fairs;
            Again if any Syracusian born
            Come to the bay of Ephesus, he dies,
            The enmity and discord which of late
            Sprang from the rancorous outrage of their Duke
            To merchants, our well-dealing countrymen,
            Who, wanting guilders to redeem their lives,
            Have sealed his rigorous statues with their bloods,
            Excludes all pity from our threatening looks.
EGEON   Proceed, Solinus, to procure my fall,
            And by the doom of death end woes all.
DUKE   Merchant of Syracusa, plead no more,
            Your goods are confiscate to my dispose,
            Unless a thousand marks be levied
            To quit the penalty and to ransom you.
            Thy, substance, valued at the highest rate,
            Cannot amount unto a hundred marks;
            Therefore by law thou art condemned to die.

2 *The Comedy of Errors* as a musical?

Here are the lyrics of the song that ended the first scene in the 1976
RSC production.

DUKE Beg thou or borrow to make up the sum
And live. If no then thou art doomed to die.
Try all the friends thou hast in Ephesus.
Gaoler take him to thy custody.

OFFICER I will my lord.

DUKE Beg thou or borrow to make up the sum,
Thou art welcome to try.
Bring not the money by set of sun, by set of sun,
Then . . . art thou doomed to die,
art thou doomed to die.

CHORUS Beg thou or borrow to make up the sum,
make up the sum, make up the sum,
Thou art welcome to try.
Bring not the money by set of sun, by set of sun,
Then . . . old man you die,
old man you die,
old man you die.

GIRLS Try all the friends thou hast in Ephesus.

DUKE Or else your story must end in Ephesus.

EGEON My comfort when your words are done,
My life ends with the evening sun.

CHORUS Beg thou or borrow to make up the sum,
make up the sum, make up the sum,
Thou art welcome to try.
But when the sun sets we beat upon the drum,
And if you come without the sum you die;
Old man you die,
Old man you die,
Old man you die,
Old man you die.

Try setting these to music, or writing your own lyrics based on part of
this scene. There is a musical based on *The Comedy of Errors* called
The Boys from Syracuse (see page 86).

The merchant returns Antipholus' money and warns him not to reveal that he is from Syracuse. Antipholus orders his servant Dromio to take the money to their inn. He invites the merchant to eat with him later.

1 Money, money, money (in pairs)

It's no coincidence that the last scene ends with the Duke urging Egeon to 'beg thou or borrow to make up the sum' of a thousand marks to free himself, and that this scene starts with a merchant. The whole play is riddled with notions of trading (both goods and roles), exchange and bargaining. Take the first two scenes, and see how many references to money and trading you can find.

2 Dramatic irony (in small groups)

The fact that Antipholus of Syracuse doesn't know the 'Syracusian merchant' is his father – but we think we do! – is an instance of **dramatic irony**. Dramatic irony is when the audience knows something that the characters don't. Here, Antipholus takes the money that could well free his father, Egeon.

Devise a scene to demonstrate dramatic irony. Show your scene to the class.

3 'I'll view the manners of the town'

Antipholus of Syracuse is like a tourist or traveller arriving in a strange place. Find out about modern-day Turkey and either:

a write the diary of someone (it could be Antipholus) arriving there for the first time, or

b travel in time and imagine you are arriving in Ephesus two thousand years ago, or

c write the journal entry for someone arriving in any new place and recording his or her first impressions, or

d write to the Turkish Tourist Board for information about resorts like Ephesus. Compile your own tourist guide to the area.

---

statute law
host stay
mean means, opportunity

mart marketplace
consort join, accompany

ACT 1   SCENE 2

Enter ANTIPHOLUS OF SYRACUSE, FIRST MERCHANT, and DROMIO OF
SYRACUSE

1 MERCHANT Therefore give out you are of Epidamnum
       Lest that your goods too soon be confiscate.
       This very day a Syracusian merchant
       Is apprehended for arrival here,
       And, not being able to buy out his life,   5
       According to the statute of the town
       Dies ere the weary sun set in the west.
       There is your money that I had to keep.
ANTIPHOLUS S. Go, bear it to the Centaur, where we host,
       And stay there, Dromio, till I come to thee.   10
       Within this hour it will be dinner-time.
       Till that I'll view the manners of the town,
       Peruse the traders, gaze upon the buildings,
       And then return and sleep within mine inn;
       For with long travel I am stiff and weary.   15
       Get thee away.
DROMIO S. Many a man would take you at your word
       And go indeed, having so good a mean.   *Exit*
ANTIPHOLUS S. A trusty villain, sir, that very oft,
       When I am dull with care and melancholy,   20
       Lightens my humour with his merry jests.
       What, will you walk with me about the town,
       And then go to my inn and dine with me?
1 MERCHANT I am invited, sir, to certain merchants,
       Of whom I hope to make much benefit.   25
       I crave your pardon. Soon at five o'clock,
       Please you, I'll meet with you upon the mart,
       And afterward consort you till bedtime.

Dromio of Ephesus enters to summon his master to eat.
Antipholus of Syracuse mistakes him for Dromio of Syracuse.
The misunderstandings begin when Antipholus asks Dromio what
he has done with the money he gave him.

1 Soliloquies (in pairs)

There are very few occasions in this play when a character is alone on stage, speaking to him- or herself (and to the audience) as in lines 33–40. Make a list of ways of directing this soliloquy on stage. Here are some ideas to give you a start:

- First two lines to himself, muttering. Rest of speech to the audience in the theatre.
- With 'voice over' – a disembodied voice coming from off-stage, representing Antipholus' thoughts.
- To another character – who?

Try these and your own ideas. Think about the *tone* of this speech: is it spoken in an unhappy way, or with humour, or . . .?

2 One thing after another!

In writing, continue the tirade in lines 44–50, in which the last item of the line serves as the beginning of the next line. Carry on from line 50.

Or using the beginning of this poem as a model, write your own piece which works in the same way:

when I missed the bus the sun came out
when I caught the sun a hat appeared
when I tossed the hat a bird flew out . . .

or continue this from Edwin Morgan's 'Sir Henry Morgan's Song':

we came to the boat and blew the horn
we blew the boom and came to the island
we came to the innocent and cut the cackle . . .
in *The New Divan*

---

confounds muddles, loses
almanac of my true date someone
  born the day I was
capon chicken

stomach appetite
crupper the strap which goes
  round a horse's hindquarters to
  keep the saddle in place

      My present business calls me from you now.

ANTIPHOLUS S. Farewell till then. I will go lose myself   30
      And wander up and down to view the city.

1 MERCHANT Sir, I commend you to your own content.   *Exit*

ANTIPHOLUS S. He that commends me to mine own content
      Commends me to the thing I cannot get.
      I to the world am like a drop of water   35
      That in the ocean seeks another drop,
      Who, falling there to find his fellow forth,
      Unseen, inquisitive, confounds himself.
      So I, to find a mother and a brother,
      In quest of them unhappy, lose myself.   40

        Enter DROMIO OF EPHESUS

      Here comes the almanac of my true date.
      What now? How chance thou art returned so soon?

DROMIO E. Returned so soon? Rather approached too late.
      The capon burns, the pig falls from the spit.
      The clock hath strucken twelve upon the bell;   45
      My mistress made it one upon my cheek.
      She is so hot because the meat is cold.
      The meat is cold because you come not home.
      You come not home because you have no stomach.
      You have no stomach, having broke your fast.   50
      But we that know what 'tis to fast and pray
      Are penitent for your default today.

ANTIPHOLUS S. Stop in your wind, sir. Tell me this, I pray:
      Where have you left the money that I gave you?

DROMIO E. O, sixpence that I had o' Wednesday last   55
      To pay the saddler for my mistress' crupper.
      The saddler had it, sir. I kept it not.

ANTIPHOLUS S. I am not in a sportive humour now.
      Tell me, and dally not: where is the money?
      We being strangers here, how dar'st thou trust   60
      So great a charge from thine own custody?

The misunderstandings continue. Antipholus begins to beat Dromio for his cheek in calling him home to dinner and for apparently losing his money.

---

1 Mistaken identity (in pairs)

Improvise a scene in which there is a case of mistaken identity. For example, you mistake one twin for another, or a young teacher for a pupil.

2 The quest for a family

You may already have written a diary entry for Antipholus' arrival in Ephesus. Write entries recording his search for his mother, father and brother around the edges of the Mediterranean Sea. Include his thoughts on this quest to find a family and an identity.

3 Costume design for Dromio

Here is John Napier's design for the 1976 RSC production. Design your own costume for the character.

---

in post post-haste, quickly
post a door post
maw stomach

stands on indulges in
undisposed not in the mood
flout mock

DROMIO E. I pray you, jest, sir, as you sit at dinner.
                    I from my mistress come to you in post.
                    If I return I shall be post indeed,
                    For she will scour your fault upon my pate.   65
                    Methinks your maw, like mine, should be your clock
                    And strike you home without a messenger.
ANTIPHOLUS S. Come, Dromio, come, these jests are out of season.
                    Reserve them till a merrier hour than this.
                    Where is the gold I gave in charge to thee?   70
DROMIO E. To me, sir? Why, you gave no gold to me.
ANTIPHOLUS S. Come on, sir knave, have done your foolishness,
                    And tell me how thou hast disposed thy charge.
DROMIO E. My charge was but to fetch you from the mart
                    Home to your house, the Phoenix, sir, to dinner.   75
                    My mistress and her sister stays for you.
ANTIPHOLUS S. Now, as I am a Christian, answer me
                    In what safe place you have bestowed my money,
                    Or I shall break that merry sconce of yours
                    That stands on tricks when I am undisposed.   80
                    Where is the thousand marks thou hadst of me?
DROMIO E. I have some marks of yours upon my pate,
                    Some of my mistress' marks upon my shoulders,
                    But not a thousand marks between you both.
                    If I should pay your worship those again,   85
                    Perchance you will not bear them patiently.
ANTIPHOLUS S. Thy mistress' marks? What mistress, slave, hast thou?
DROMIO E. Your worship's wife, my mistress at the Phoenix;
                    She that doth fast till you come home to dinner,
                    And prays that you will hie you home to dinner.   90
ANTIPHOLUS S.   What, wilt thou flout me thus unto my face,
                    Being forbid? There, take you that, sir knave.
                                    [*He beats Dromio*]
DROMIO E. What mean you, sir? For God's sake hold your hands.
                    Nay, an you will not, sir, I'll take my heels.   *Exit*

Antipholus of Syracuse, fearful of the deceits of Ephesus, worries about his money. Adriana wonders why Antipholus of Ephesus is late for dinner.

1 Corrupt Ephesus! (in groups of two or three)

In lines 95–105, Antipholus of Syracuse tells the audience what he has heard about Ephesus. This is no ordinary town, but one that is deeply corrupt. Using this speech as your guide, create mimes of each aspect of life in Ephesus ('nimble jugglers', 'dark-working sorcerers' etc.), showing rather than telling of the town's activities. All the mimes can be presented together, with Antipholus wandering from group to group in bemused/fearful/cautious fashion. Use moments of 'freeze-frame' (a still photograph) to talk together about what they show you about life in Ephesus.

2 Men and women (in groups of four)

'Why should their liberty than ours be more?' (line 10)

To what extent do you agree or disagree with the following statements:

- 'a man is master of his liberty'
- women should obey their husbands
- men are less free to do what they like than women
- most women don't feel in control of their own liberty
- women are more free outside marriage than they are inside it
- men should always tell their wives where they are
- men are more free 'because their business still lies out o' door'.

3 From blank verse into rhyme (in pairs)

Most of the play is in blank (unrhymed) verse, but somewhere in Scene 1 opposite, the speeches shift into rhyming couplets. Read the scene aloud to identify where that shift takes place. When you have worked out how long the rhyming couplets go on, talk together about why you think Shakespeare decided to write this section in rhyme.

---

is o'er-raught has tricked me
cozenage cheating
prating mountebanks so-called
  doctors quacking about their cures

still always
bound boundary

ANTIPHOLUS S. Upon my life, by some device or other   95
    The villain is o'er-raught of all my money.
    They say this town is full of cozenage,
    As nimble jugglers that deceive the eye,
    Dark-working sorcerers that change the mind,
    Soul-killing witches that deform the body,   100
    Disguisèd cheaters, prating mountebanks,
    And many suchlike liberties of sin.
    If it prove so, I will be gone the sooner.
    I'll to the Centaur to go seek this slave.
    I greatly fear my money is not safe.   *Exit*   105

ACT 2   SCENE 1

Enter ADRIANA, wife to ANTIPHOLUS OF EPHESUS,
with LUCIANA, her sister

ADRIANA Neither my husband nor the slave returned,
    That in such haste I sent to seek his master?
    Sure, Luciana, it is two o'clock.
LUCIANA Perhaps some merchant hath invited him,
    And from the mart he's somewhere gone to dinner.   5
    Good sister, let us dine, and never fret.
    A man is master of his liberty;
    Time is their master, and when they see time
    They'll go or come. If so, be patient, sister.
ADRIANA Why should their liberty than ours be more?   10
LUCIANA   Because their business still lies out o'door.
ADRIANA Look, when I serve him so, he takes it ill.
LUCIANA O, know he is the bridle of your will.
ADRIANA There's none but asses will be bridled so.
LUCIANA Why, headstrong liberty is lashed with woe.   15
    There's nothing situate under heaven's eye
    But hath his bound in earth, in sea, in sky.

Luciana declares that women must obey their men, and be patient. Adriana thinks Luciana would not be as patient if she were married. Dromio returns to report the blows he has received at the hands of Antipholus.

1 The chain of being (in pairs)

Lines 16–24 relate to the great 'chain of being' that many Elizabethan people believed explained the order and hierarchy of creatures and other things in the universe. Here are some links in that chain: birds, animals, humankind, stones, angels, God. Using the script as a guide, put them in the right order according to the Elizabethan belief. Then rearrange the list according to *your* perception of the relationship between them.

Talk together about how far you agree with Luciana's views in lines 16–24. Are men 'masters to their females'?

2 Who's who?

A photograph from the Royal Shakespeare Company's 1990 production. Identify Adriana. Which lines best fit this moment?

Names: Adriana suggests 'dark lady' (Latin 'ater') and Luciana 'light lady' (Latin 'lux'). Does this match your view of the two sisters?

indued supplied
accords consents
bear some sway have some
  authority

though she pause if she pauses (to
  consider marriage)
like right bereft similar theft of
  your rights
doubtfully dreadfully

The beasts, the fishes, and the wingèd fowls
Are their males' subjects, and at their controls.
Man, more divine, the master of all these,   20
Lord of the wide world and wild watery seas,
Indued with intellectual sense and souls,
Of more pre-eminence than fish and fowls,
Are masters to their females, and their lords.
Then let your will attend on their accords.   25

ADRIANA This servitude makes you to keep unwed.
LUCIANA Not this, but troubles of the marriage-bed.
ADRIANA But were you wedded, you would bear some sway.
LUCIANA Ere I learn love, I'll practise to obey.
ADRIANA How if your husband start some otherwhere?   30
LUCIANA Till he come home again, I would forbear.
ADRIANA Patience unmoved! No marvel though she pause.
       They can be meek that have no other cause.
       A wretched soul, bruised with adversity,
       We bid be quiet when we hear it cry.   35
       But were we burdened with like weight of pain,
       As much or more we should ourselves complain.
       So thou, that hast no unkind mate to grieve thee,
       With urging helpless patience would relieve me.
       But if thou live to see like right bereft,   40
       This fool-begged patience in thee will be left.
LUCIANA Well, I will marry one day, but to try.
       Here comes your man. Now is your husband nigh.

Enter DROMIO [OF] EPHESUS

ADRIANA Say, is your tardy master now at hand?
DROMIO E. Nay, he's at two hands with me, and that my two ears can   45
       witness.
ADRIANA Say, didst thou speak with him? Know'st thou his mind?
DROMIO E. Ay, ay, he told his mind upon mine ear.
       Beshrew his hand, I scarce could understand it.
LUCIANA Spake he so doubtfully, thou couldst not feel his meaning?   50
DROMIO E. Nay, he struck so plainly, I could too well feel his blows, and
       withal so doubtfully that I could scarce understand them.

*Dromio tells more of how Antipholus denies having anything
to do with Adriana. She orders him to bring Antipholus home, and
beats him soundly to enforce her command.*

1 '"My gold", quoth he' (in pairs)

First, act out lines 60–5. Then write a short story or a playscript in
which one character repeats a single word, phrase or sentence.

2 The fool: yesterday and today

List as many characteristics as you
can think of that belong to fools and
clowns. Include the names of any
clowns or fools you can remember
(including from film or television).
Which characteristics apply to the
Dromios?

An Elizabethan fool,
Richard Tarleton.

horn-mad passionately angry,
  sexually 'horny'
cuckold a husband whose wife is
  having an affair. Cuckolds wore
  'horns'

**my errand, due unto my
  tongue** the message that I should
  have carried on my tongue
round outspoken
spurn kick

ADRIANA But say, I prithee, is he coming home?
      It seems he hath great care to please his wife.
DROMIO E. Why, mistress, sure my master is horn-mad.   55
ADRIANA Horn-mad, thou villain?
DROMIO E.   I mean not cuckold-mad,
      But sure he is stark mad.
      When I desired him to come home to dinner
      He asked me for a thousand marks in gold.
      ''Tis dinner-time', quoth I. 'My gold', quoth he.   60
      'Your meat doth burn', quoth I. 'My gold', quoth he.
      'Will you come home?' quoth I. 'My gold', quoth he.
      'Where is the thousand marks I gave thee, villain?'
      'The pig', quoth I, 'is burned.' 'My gold', quoth he.
      'My mistress, sir –' quoth I. 'Hang up thy mistress!   65
      I know not thy mistress. Out on thy mistress!'
LUCIANA Quoth who?
DROMIO E. Quoth my master.
      'I know', quoth he, 'no house, no wife, no mistress.'
      So that my errand, due unto my tongue,   70
      I thank him, I bare home upon my shoulders;
      For, in conclusion, he did beat me there.
ADRIANA Go back again, thou slave, and fetch him home.
DROMIO E. Go back again and be new-beaten home?
      For God's sake send some other messenger.   75
ADRIANA Back, slave, or I will break thy pate across.
DROMIO E. And he will bless that cross with other beating,
      Between you I shall have a holy head.
ADRIANA Hence, prating peasant, fetch thy master home.
                      [She beats Dromio]
DROMIO E. Am I so round with you as you with me   80
      That like a football you do spurn me thus?
      You spurn me hence, and he will spurn me hither.
      If I last in this service you must case me in leather.   *[Exit]*

Adriana complains that she is made to seem dull and unattractive because Antipholus is such a gadabout. Luciana accuses her sister of jealousy. Adriana insists Antipholus no longer loves her.

1 'How many fond fools serve mad jealousy!'
(in groups of four)

Improvise a scene that explores feelings of jealousy.

2 Jealousy

Here is the beginning of a pamphlet on jealousy, published in 1593 – about the time when *The Comedy of Errors* was written.

> In the country of Every-place he raigneth, as ruler as pernitious (i.e. pernicious – malevolent, evil) as mighty, and more mighty than either vertuous or peaceable. As his kingdom is large, so his subjectes are many, his land being inhabited by people no less unruely than himselfe . . . Many are his adversaries and more his friends, every disposition drawn to follow his humours (states of mind, moods) and desirous of his entertainment. His chiefest citty and seat of pleasure . . . stands on top of a high hill called Mistrustfulnesse, at foot whereof runneth the swift river called Unconstancy . . .
>
> from *Tell-Trothes New-Yeares Gift*

Continue this portrait of jealousy, writing about the trophies, successes, physical postures, goods, defence armoury and games played in this kingdom.

3 Difficult lines

Lines 105–11 are notoriously difficult. Write your own clear modern English version, then compare notes with a partner. Who in the class can read the most satisfactory version – or act it?

---

minions mistresses
discourses conversation
defeatures ugliness
fair beauty

pale fence
stale harlot
fond silly, infatuated

LUCIANA Fie, how impatience loureth in your face.

ADRIANA His company must do his minions grace   85
    Whilst I at home starve for a merry look.
    Hath homely age th'alluring beauty took
    From my poor cheek? Then he hath wasted it.
    Are my discourses dull? barren my wit?
    If voluble and sharp discourse be marred,   90
    Unkindness blunts it more than marble hard.
    Do their gay vestments his affections bait?
    That's not my fault; he's master of my state.
    What ruins are in me that can be found
    By him not ruined? Then is he the ground   95
    Of my defeatures. My decayèd fair
    A sunny look of his would soon repair.
    But, too unruly deer, he breaks the pale
    And feeds from home. Poor I am but his stale.

LUCIANA Self-harming jealousy! Fie, beat it hence.   100

ADRIANA Unfeeling fools can with such wrongs dispense.
    I know his eye doth homage otherwhere;
    Or else what lets it but he would be here?
    Sister, you know he promised me a chain.
    Would that alone a love him would detain   105
    So he would keep fair quarter with his bed.
    I see the jewel best enamellèd
    Will lose his beauty. Yet the gold bides still
    That others touch; and often touching will
    Wear gold, and no man that hath a name   110
    But falsehood and corruption doth it shame.
    Since that my beauty cannot please his eye,
    I'll weep what's left away, and weeping die.

LUCIANA How many fond fools serve mad jealousy!

Exeunt

Antipholus of Syracuse is relieved to find his gold is safe. His servant Dromio reappears, and is mystified by Antipholus' questions. Thinking his servant cheeky, Antipholus beats him, unaware there are two Dromios.

1 'The gold I gave to Dromio is laid up . . .' (in pairs)

Imagine that this first speech (lines 1–6) of Antipholus was left out. Would it matter?

2 Two Dromios or one? (in small groups)

Below is a photograph of the two Dromios in a 1953 production. But in the 1990 RSC production of *The Comedy of Errors*, both Dromios were played by one actor, and both Antipholuses by one actor. Talk together about the advantages and disadvantages of such an arrangement.

computation working out
strokes blows
merry vein good humour

ACT 2   SCENE 2

Enter ANTIPHOLUS OF SYRACUSE

ANTIPHOLUS S. The gold I gave to Dromio is laid up
　　　　　Safe at the Centaur, and the heedful slave
　　　　　Is wandered forth in care to seek me out
　　　　　By computation and mine host's report.
　　　　　I could not speak with Dromio since at first　　　　5
　　　　　I sent him from the mart. See, here he comes.

Enter DROMIO OF SYRACUSE

　　　　　How now, sir. Is your merry humour altered?
　　　　　As you love strokes, so jest with me again.
　　　　　You know no Centaur? You received no gold?
　　　　　Your mistress sent to have me home to dinner?　　10
　　　　　My house was at the Phoenix? Wast thou mad
　　　　　That thus so madly thou didst answer me?
DROMIO S. What answer, sir? When spake I such a word?
ANTIPHOLUS S. Even now, even here, not half an hour since.
DROMIO S. I did not see you since you sent me hence　　　15
　　　　　Home to the Centaur with the gold you gave me.
ANTIPHOLUS S. Villain, thou didst deny the gold's receipt,
　　　　　And told'st me of a mistress and a dinner,
　　　　　For which I hope thou felt'st I was displeased.
DROMIO S. I am glad to see you in this merry vein.　　　20
　　　　　What means this jest? I pray you, master, tell me.
ANTIPHOLUS S. Yea, dost thou jeer and flout me in the teeth?
　　　　　Think'st thou I jest? Hold, take thou that, and that.
　　　　　　　　　　[He] beats Dromio

Antipholus continues to scold Dromio for jesting when he wasn't in the mood for it. Dromio responds with witty word-play.

---

1 Beatings (in pairs)

How are these beatings to be acted without actually hurting the other character? Without touching each other experiment with various ways of carrying out the beatings. Work out a comic sequence, using the lines in the script.

2 Reacting to someone else's mood (in groups of four)

'fashion your demeanour to my looks' (line 33)

Improvise some short scenes in which one character's mood determines the way the other characters behave in relation to him or her. Include rapid shifts of mood so that the other characters have to adapt to the new situations.

3 'There's a time for all things' (in groups of three or four)

Work out a scene that leads towards this statement (line 60) spoken by one of the characters near or at the end of the scene.

---

bargain agreement
aspect mood
sconce head, small fort, protective
  screen
flouting mocking

wants lacks
basting covering meat with fat
  during cooking; and a beating – a
  typical Shakespearean pun
choleric hot-tempered

DROMIO S. Hold, sir, for God's sake; now your jest is earnest.
    Upon what bargain do you give it me?   25
ANTIPHOLUS S. Because that I familiarly sometimes
    Do use you for my fool, and chat with you,
    Your sauciness will jest upon my love,
    And make a common of my serious hours.
    When the sun shines let foolish gnats make sport,   30
    But creep in crannies when he hides his beams.
    If you will jest with me, know my aspect,
    And fashion your demeanour to my looks,
    Or I will beat this method in your sconce.
DROMIO S. 'Sconce' call you it? So you would leave battering I had rather   35
have it a head. And you use these blows long I must get a sconce for
my head, and ensconce it too, or else I shall seek my wit in my
shoulders. But I pray, sir, why am I beaten?
ANTIPHOLUS S. Dost thou not know?
DROMIO S. Nothing, sir, but that I am beaten.   40
ANTIPHOLUS S. Shall I tell you why?
DROMIO S. Ay, sir, and wherefore; for they say every why hath a
wherefore.
ANTIPHOLUS S. Why, first for flouting me; and then wherefore –
    For urging it the second time to me.   45
DROMIO S. Was there ever any man thus beaten out of season,
    When in the why and the wherefore is neither rhyme nor reason?
    Well, sir, I thank you.
ANTIPHOLUS S.   Thank me, sir, for what?
DROMIO S. Marry, sir, for this something that you gave me for nothing.
ANTIPHOLUS S. I'll make you amends next, to give you nothing for   50
something. But say, sir, is it dinner-time?
DROMIO S. No, sir. I think the meat wants that I have.
ANTIPHOLUS S. In good time, sir, what's that?
DROMIO Basting.
ANTIPHOLUS S. Well, sir, then 'twill be dry.   55
DROMIO S. If it be, sir, I pray you eat none of it.
ANTIPHOLUS S. Your reason?
DROMIO S. Lest it make you choleric, and purchase me another dry
basting.
ANTIPHOLUS S. Well, sir, learn to jest in good time. There's a time for all   60
things.

Antipholus and Dromio continue their repartee, on the theme of baldness.

---

1 'I durst have denied that before you were so choleric'
(in groups of four)

'Choleric' (line 62) means passionate, full of bile (venom), angry, irascible. It was considered by the Elizabethans as one of the four 'humours' or types of character and behaviour, the others being phlegmatic, melancholic and sanguine. Create scenes in which each character adopts one of the humours and acts accordingly.

Sanguine: confident, inclined to hopefulness.

Melancholic: miserable, depressed.

Choleric: angry, bilious.

Phlegmatic: cold and sluggish.

---

by fine and recovery legal terms to do with the transferring of property
fine for a periwig fee for a wig
excrement something growing from the body

scanted been stingy to
tiring attiring (combing his hair)
bald 'trivial' as well as 'without hair'

DROMIO S. I durst have denied that before you were so choleric.

ANTIPHOLUS S. By what rule, sir?

DROMIO S. Marry, sir, by a rule as plain as the plain bald pate of Father
   Time himself.   65

ANTIPHOLUS S. Let's hear it.

DROMIO S. There's no time for a man to recover his hair that grows bald
   by nature.

ANTIPHOLUS S. May he not do it by fine and recovery?

DROMIO S. Yes, to pay a fine for a periwig, and recover the lost hair of   70
   another man.

ANTIPHOLUS S. Why is Time such a niggard of hair, being, as it is, so
   plentiful an excrement?

DROMIO S. Because it is a blessing that he bestows on beasts, and what he
   hath scanted men in hair he hath given them in wit.   75

ANTIPHOLUS S. Why, but there's many a man hath more hair than wit.

DROMIO S. Not a man of those but he hath the wit to lose his hair.

ANTIPHOLUS S. Why, thou didst conclude hairy men plain dealers,
   without wit.

DROMIO S. The plainer dealer, the sooner lost; yet he loseth it in a kind of 80
   jollity.

ANTIPHOLUS S. For what reason?

DROMIO S. For two, and sound ones too.

ANTIPHOLUS S. Nay, not sound, I pray you.

DROMIO S. Sure ones, then.   85

ANTIPHOLUS S. Nay, not sure in a thing falsing.

DROMIO S. Certain ones, then.

ANTIPHOLUS S. Name them.

DROMIO S. The one, to save the money that he spends in tiring; the
   other, that at dinner they should not drop in his porridge.   90

ANTIPHOLUS S. You would all this time have proved there is no time for
   all things.

DROMIO S. Marry, and did, sir; namely, e'en no time to recover hair lost
   by nature.

ANTIPHOLUS S. But your reason was not substantial, why there is no   95
   time to recover.

DROMIO S. Thus I mend it: Time himself is bald, and therefore to the
   world's end will have bald followers.

ANTIPHOLUS S. I knew 'twould be a bald conclusion. But soft, who wafts
   us yonder?   100

33

*Adriana addresses herself to Antipholus of Syracuse, declaring herself
his loyal wife despite all his (supposed) infidelities. She is so close to him that
she has been tainted by some of his 'disease' of adultery.*

1 Approaches to reading the speech (in pairs)

Sit opposite each other. Read one line each, in turn, throughout the
speech. Read it again, this time reading a sentence each at a time.
Then break the speech into longer sections, and read again, sharing
the sections as you think appropriate.

2 Rearranging the sequence of the speech
(in groups of four to five)

Write each sentence of the speech on separate pieces of paper, for
example, 'I am not Adriana, nor thy wife' and 'Keep then fair league
and truce with thy true bed, I live unstained, thou undishonoured'.
Shuffle the papers. Without looking back at the script, try to
reconstruct the speech in the order it appears here. Experiment with
different sequences, such as all the longest sentences together, and all
the shortest together – and so on. Which sequence do you find most
satisfactory?

3 Rewriting parts of the speech

Take two sentences of the speech and replace them with two of your
own. Make them sound like Shakespeare and fit in with Adriana's
mood as an outraged wife. Then read or record the speech to see if
anyone can spot your insertions.

4 Advice to an actress (in pairs)

Make notes of your advice to an actress on how to perform the
speech. What reactions should she expect from the others on stage,
especially Antipholus?

---

incorporate without a body
licentious promiscuous (sleeping
  around)
adulterate blot the stain of
  adultery

strumpeted made a prostitute
contagion disease
league and truce union and peace

Enter ADRIANA *and* LUCIANA

ADRIANA Ay, ay, Antipholus, look strange and frown;
　　　　Some other mistress hath thy sweet aspects.
　　　　I am not Adriana, nor thy wife.
　　　　The time was once when thou unurged wouldst vow
　　　　That never words were music to thine ear,　　　　　105
　　　　That never object pleasing in thine eye,
　　　　That never touch well welcome to thy hand,
　　　　That never meat sweet-savoured in thy taste,
　　　　Unless I spake, or looked, or touched, or carved to thee.
　　　　How comes it now, my husband, O, how comes it,　　110
　　　　That thou art then estrangèd from thyself?
　　　　Thyself I call it, being strange to me
　　　　That undividable, incorporate,
　　　　Am better than thy dear self's better part.
　　　　Ah, do not tear away thyself from me;　　　　　　115
　　　　For know, my love, as easy mayst thou fall
　　　　A drop of water in the breaking gulf,
　　　　And take unmingled thence that drop again
　　　　Without addition or diminishing,
　　　　As take from me thyself, and not me too.　　　　　120
　　　　How dearly would it touch thee to the quick
　　　　Shouldst thou but hear I were licentious,
　　　　And that this body, consecrate to thee,
　　　　By ruffian lust should be contaminate?
　　　　Wouldst thou not spit at me, and spurn at me,　　125
　　　　And hurl the name of husband in my face,
　　　　And tear the stained skin off my harlot brow,
　　　　And from my false hand cut the wedding ring,
　　　　And break it with a deep-divorcing vow?
　　　　I know thou canst, and therefore see thou do it.　　130
　　　　I am possessed with an adulterate blot.
　　　　My blood is mingled with the crime of lust;
　　　　For if we two be one, and thou play false,
　　　　I do digest the poison of thy flesh,
　　　　Being strumpeted by thy contagion.　　　　　　135
　　　　Keep then fair league and truce with thy true bed,
　　　　I live unstained, thou undishonourèd.

Antipholus is amazed by Adriana's attentions. The confusion continues, with Dromio being accused of lying. Antipholus begins to accept the idea of being wooed by Adriana.

1 'Plead you to me, fair dame?' (in pairs)

How many different ways can you think of to make the audience laugh at line 138? Take into account what Antipholus has been doing during the previous long speech by Adriana, and how he is going to deliver this line. Perform your version of lines 132–8.

2 Another case of mistaken identity! (in groups of three)

Adriana believes she is talking with her husband, Antipholus of Ephesus. Antipholus of Syracuse is confused by her. Dromio, caught in between them, is mistaken for the other Dromio (of Ephesus). Invent a similar situation involving three characters: one of you is convinced of a past connection with the others, but the other two are not so sure.

3 Asides (in groups of three or four)

Create a short scene involving mistaken identity (it could be as 2 above). Include asides from one or all of the characters. Or, in groups of four, set up a dialogue between two characters while the other two speak the real thoughts of the two main characters. These 'shadow' voices – rather like the inner self speaking – can be located just behind the actual participants in the dialogue.

4 *Alter egos* (in groups of four or eight)

Using the same technique as in 3 above, give each of the four characters in lines 138–71 an *alter ego* ('the other self'). Each *alter ego* speaks the character's private feelings after each 'public' speech.

---

course and drift of your
  compact the nature and direction
  of your plot
abetting backing him up
wrong not . . . contempt don't
  make that fault worse by heaping
  on more contempt

possess thee take you away from
dross scum, waste
theme the subject of her speech
fallacy delusion, mistake

ANTIPHOLUS S. Plead you to me, fair dame? I know you not.
    In Ephesus I am but two hours old,
    As strange unto your town as to your talk,   140
    Who, every word by all my wit being scanned,
    Wants wit in all one word to understand.
LUCIANA Fie, brother, how the world is changed with you.
    When were you wont to use my sister thus?
    She sent for you by Dromio home to dinner.   145
ANTIPHOLUS S. By Dromio?
DROMIO S. By me?
ADRIANA By thee; and this thou didst return from him,
    That he did buffet thee, and in his blows
    Denied my house for his, me for his wife.   150
ANTIPHOLUS S. Did you converse, sir, with this gentlewoman?
    What is the course and drift of your compact?
DROMIO S. I, sir? I never saw her till this time.
ANTIPHOLUS S. Villain, thou liest, for even her very words
    Didst thou deliver to me on the mart.   155
DROMIO S. I never spake with her in all my life.
ANTIPHOLUS S. How can she thus then call us by our names –
    Unless it be by inspiration?
ADRIANA How ill agrees it with your gravity
    To counterfeit thus grossly with your slave,   160
    Abetting him to thwart me in my mood.
    Be it my wrong, you are from me exempt;
    But wrong not that wrong with a more contempt.
    Come, I will fasten on this sleeve of thine.
    Thou art an elm, my husband, I a vine,   165
    Whose weakness, married to thy stronger state,
    Makes me with thy strength to communicate.
    If aught possess thee from me, it is dross,
    Usurping ivy, briar, or idle moss,
    Who, all for want of pruning, with intrusion   170
    Infect thy sap, and live on thy confusion.
ANTIPHOLUS S. [*Aside*] To me she speaks; she moves me for her theme.
    What, was I married to her in my dream?
    Or sleep I now, and think I hear all this?
    What error drives our eyes and ears amiss?   175
    Until I know this sure uncertainty,
    I'll entertain the offered fallacy.

*Both Antipholus and Dromio think they are in some kind of fairyland,
but they decide to go along with it. Antipholus goes to dine with Adriana,
while Dromio guards the gate.*

1 'This is the fairy land' (in pairs)

Devise ways in which the effect of being in a dream, or of thinking
you are in 'fairyland', can be created on stage. Use voices, movements, lighting and other devices. Take line 181 as a beginning, but
add other dream elements. Try some of these effects at particular
points towards the end of the scene. Do they work, or do they add too
much of an element of romance and mystique to the comic action?

2 The story so far (in small groups)

So far there have been four scenes. Devise a single tableau to catch the
essence of each scene. Present the sequence to the rest of the class

> **or** choose one phrase, line or sentence from each scene to convey
> the character of the play
>
> **or** script and present a short television or radio news programme
> on events in the Mediterranean and in particular, in Ephesus.

sot drunkard
long for grass look forward to
  retirement
shrive hear confession and free you
  from
persever keep striving

LUCIANA Dromio, go bid the servants spread for dinner.

DROMIO S. [*Aside*] O for my beads! I cross me for a sinner.
       This is the fairy land. O spite of spites,   180
       We talk with goblins, owls, and sprites;
       If we obey them not, this will ensue:
       They'll suck our breath, or pinch us black and blue.

LUCIANA Why prat'st thou to thyself, and answer'st not?
       Dromio, thou Dromio, thou snail, thou slug, thou sot.   185

DROMIO S. I am transformèd, master, am not I?

ANTIPHOLUS S. I think thou art in mind, and so am I.

DROMIO S. Nay, master, both in mind and in my shape.

ANTIPHOLUS S. Thou hast thine own form.

DROMIO S.   No, I am an ape.

LUCIANA If thou art changed to aught, 'tis to an ass.   190

DROMIO S. 'Tis true, she rides me, and I long for grass.
       'Tis so, I am an ass, else it could never be
       But I should know her as well as she knows me.

ADRIANA Come, come, no longer will I be a fool,
       To put the finger in the eye and weep   195
       Whilst man and master laughs my woes to scorn.
       Come, sir, to dinner. Dromio, keep the gate.
       Husband, I'll dine above with you today,
       And shrive you of a thousand idle pranks.
       Sirrah, if any ask you for your master,   200
       Say he dines forth, and let no creature enter.
       Come, sister. Dromio, play the porter well.

ANTIPHOLUS S. [*Aside*] Am I in earth, in heaven, or in hell?
       Sleeping or waking? mad or well advised?
       Known unto these, and to myself disguised?   205
       I'll say as they say, and persever so,
       And in this mist at all adventures go.

DROMIO S. Master, shall I be porter at the gate?

ADRIANA Ay, and let none enter, lest I break your pate.

LUCIANA Come, come, Antipholus, we dine too late.   210

                                     [*Exeunt*]

Looking back at Acts 1 and 2

1 A missing scene (in small groups)

We don't actually see the scene in which Adriana and Antipholus of Syracuse have dinner. Based on the evidence of the last few scenes, and using the illustrations opposite of wealthy Elizabethan families at supper, script, plan and act or improvise the missing scene.

You will have to decide:

a whether Luciana is present at the table
b how Adriana and Antipholus will behave
c whether the woman and her 'husband' will be served at table.

Other material to bear in mind:

- the conversation on jealousy (see page 27)
- Antipholus' resolve to 'entertain the offered fallacy' even though he's not sure whether he is 'in earth, in heaven or in hell'
- this extract from the Bible (St Paul's Epistle [letter] to the Christians in Ephesus). Many readers of the play think this provides important background to the themes and issues of *The Comedy of Errors*:

Wives, be subject to your husbands, as to the Lord. For the husband is the head of the wife as Christ is the head of the church, his body, and is himself its Saviour. As the church is subject to Christ, so let wives be subject in everything to their husbands. Husbands, love your wives, as Christ loved the church and gave himself up for her, that he might sanctify her, having cleansed her by the washing of water with the word, that he might present the church to himself in splendour, without spot or wrinkle or any such thing, that she might be holy and without blemish. Even so husbands should love their wives as their own bodies. He who loves his wife loves himself, for no man ever hates his own flesh, but nourishes and cherishes it.

Before embarking on the writing of your missing scene, discuss the issue of a woman's position in relation to her husband.

2 Shortening the first scene

Imagine you are directing the play. You decide to cut some of the lines, reducing the first scene from 158 to under 100 lines. Which lines would you cut? You can rearrange as well as cut lines.

3 *Othello* (in pairs)

Another Shakespeare play in which jealousy plays an important part is the tragedy *Othello*. In it, a black general is made to feel jealous of his white wife, Desdemona. He thinks that she is having an affair with Cassio, his lieutenant. Desdemona tries in vain to convince him of her faithfulness.

Enact a scene in which Antipholus of Ephesus answers the sentences of Adriana (2.1.85–113) with angry and/or peace-making statements of his own.

Elizabethan dining scenes.

Antipholus of Ephesus scolds his Dromio for accusing him of a beating in the market-place. Antipholus invites the merchant Balthasar and the goldsmith Angelo to his house. They talk about hospitality.

1 Different ways of speaking the opening speech (in pairs)

Should lines 1–10 be spoken in an angry tone throughout, or lightly and humorously? Or in some other style? Experiment until you find a way of speaking that you think suits the speech.

2 A designer's problem (in small groups)

This is the first time we have seen Antipholus of Ephesus. Talk together about ways in which a costume designer of a stage production can signal to the audience that this is not Antipholus of Syracuse. Then design the costumes for the twins.

3 What's the difference?

As you read and act the following scenes, note the differences between Antipholus of Ephesus and Antipholus of Syracuse. Set them out as follows. Include quotations from the play where they reveal something particular about each of the characters.

Antipholus of Ephesus	Antipholus of Syracuse
Confident Angry 'My wife is shrewish when I keep not hours'	Bemused Worried 'In Ephesus I am but two hours old'

carcanet jewelled necklace (the chain)
face me down out-stare me, make me a liar
at that pass in such a position

churl peasant
cheer fare
cates food and drink

ACT 3   SCENE 1

Enter ANTIPHOLUS OF EPHESUS, *his man* DROMIO, ANGELO *the goldsmith and* BALTHASAR *the merchant*

ANTIPHOLUS E. Good Signior Angelo, you must excuse us all.
My wife is shrewish when I keep not hours.
Say that I lingered with you at your shop
To see the making of her carcanet,
And that tomorrow you will bring it home.   5
But here's a villain that would face me down
He met me on the mart, and that I beat him,
And charged him with a thousand marks in gold,
And that I did deny my wife and house.
Thou drunkard, thou, what didst thou mean by this?   10

DROMIO E. Say what you will, sir, but I know what I know:
That you beat me at the mart I have your hand to show.
If the skin were parchment and the blows you gave were ink,
Your own handwriting would tell you what I think.
ANTIPHOLUS E. I think thou art an ass.
DROMIO E.   Marry, so it doth appear   15
By the wrongs I suffer, and the blows I bear.
I should kick, being kicked, and, being at that pass,
You would keep from my heels, and beware of an ass.
ANTIPHOLUS E. You're sad, Signior Balthasar. Pray God our cheer
May answer my good will, and your good welcome here.   20
BALTHASAR I hold your dainties cheap, sir, and your welcome dear.
ANTIPHOLUS E. O, Signior Balthasar, either at flesh or fish
A table full of welcome makes scarce one dainty dish.
BALTHASAR Good meat, sir, is common. That every churl affords.
ANTIPHOLUS E. And welcome more common, for that's nothing but   25
          words.
BALTHASAR Small cheer and great welcome makes a merry feast.
ANTIPHOLUS E. Ay, to a niggardly host and more sparing guest.
But though my cates be mean, take them in good part.
Better cheer may you have, but not with better heart.
But soft, my door is locked. Go bid them let us in.   30

Antipholus of Ephesus and his Dromio find the door of their house locked, with Dromio of Syracuse installed as porter. They become increasingly angry as Luce refuses them entry.

1 'Go, get thee from the door' (in pairs)

Sketch how you picture this situation (line 35) being seen by an audience. Would you have them view it in profile, with both Dromio of Syracuse (inside the house) and Dromio and Antipholus of Ephesus (outside) in full view? Or would the audience only see part of the first Dromio at the 'hatch' or through some other gaps in the door or wall? Are all characters on the same level? How would you set it in a space somewhere in your school? Join with two other pairs to compare notes and agree a plan for the enactment of the scene. What does the stage direction '*above*' imply?

2 Act the scene (in groups of six)

First, cast the characters in order of appearance: Dromio of Ephesus, Dromio of Syracuse, Antipholus of Ephesus, Luce (Adriana's kitchen-maid), Angelo and Balthasar. Rehearse the scene. Show it to the rest of the class.

3 Let me in! (in groups of three)

Improvise a scene based on someone being refused entry to his or her own house.

mome blockhead
capon a castrated cockerel
coxcomb fools sometimes wore cock's combs . . .
patch . . . and patches

mickle great
coil disturbance
shall I set in my staff? shall I set myself up here?
minion hussy

DROMIO E. Maud, Bridget, Marian, Cicely, Gillian, Ginn!

DROMIO S. [*Within*] Mome, malthorse, capon, coxcomb, idiot, patch,
    Either get thee from the door or sit down at the hatch.
    Dost thou conjure for wenches, that thou callest for such store,
    When one is one too many? Go, get thee from the door.   35

DROMIO E. What patch is made our porter? My master stays in the
    street.

DROMIO S. [*Within*] Let him walk from whence he came, lest he catch
    cold on's feet.

ANTIPHOLUS E. Who talks within, there? Ho, open the door.

DROMIO S. [*Within*] Right, sir, I'll tell you when and you'll tell me
    wherefore.

ANTIPHOLUS E. Wherefore? For my dinner. I have not dined today.   40

DROMIO S. [*Within*] Nor today here you must not. Come again when
    you may.

ANTIPHOLUS E. What art thou that keepest me out from the house I
    owe?

DROMIO S. [*Within*] The porter for this time, sir, and my name is
    Dromio.

DROMIO E. O, villain, thou hast stolen both mine office and my name.
    The one ne'er got me credit, the other mickle blame.   45
    If thou hadst been Dromio today in my place,
    Thou wouldst have changed thy face for a name, or thy name
    for an ass.

Enter LUCE [*above*]

LUCE What a coil is there, Dromio! Who are those at the gate?

DROMIO E. Let my master in, Luce.

LUCE   Faith, no, he comes too late,
    And so tell your master.

DROMIO E.   O lord, I must laugh.   50
    Have at you with a proverb: 'Shall I set in my staff?'

LUCE Have at you with another. That's 'When? Can you tell?'

DROMIO S. [*Within*] If thy name be called Luce, Luce, thou hast
    answered him well.

ANTIPHOLUS E. Do you hear, you minion? You'll let us in, I trow.

LUCE I thought to have asked you.

DROMIO S. [*Within*]   And you said no.   55

DROMIO E. So come – help. Well struck! There was blow for blow.

Adriana dismisses her real husband, Antipholus of Ephesus, from the door.
After insulting exchanges between the two Dromios, Antipholus resolves to
knock the door down with a crowbar.

1 Who's who?

Identify the characters in these production photographs (from the
1984 Royal Shakespeare Company revival and the 1966 Royal
Lyceum Theatre, Edinburgh production). Find the lines at which
each of these moments takes place.

ANTIPHOLUS E. Thou baggage, let me in.
LUCE   Can you tell for whose sake?
DROMIO E. Master, knock the door hard.
LUCE   Let him knock till it ache.
ANTIPHOLUS E. You'll cry for this, minion, if I beat the door down.
LUCE What needs all that, and a pair of stocks in the town?   60

Enter ADRIANA [*above*]

ADRIANA Who is that at the door that keeps all this noise?
DROMIO S. [*Within*] By my troth, your town is troubled with unruly
        boys.
ANTIPHOLUS E. Are you there, wife? You might have come before.
ADRIANA Your wife, sir knave? Go get you from the door.
                                    [*Exit with Luce*]
DROMIO E. If you went in pain, master, this knave would go sore.   65
ANGELO Here is neither cheer, sir, nor welcome. We would fain have
        either.
BALTHASAR In debating which was best, we shall part with neither.
DROMIO E. They stand at the door, master. Bid them welcome hither.
ANTIPHOLUS E. There is something in the wind, that we cannot get in.
DROMIO E. You would say so, master, if your garments were thin.   70
        Your cake is warm within. You stand here in the cold.
        It would make a man mad as a buck to be so bought and sold.
ANTIPHOLUS E. Go fetch me something. I'll break ope the gate.
DROMIO S. [*Within*] Break any breaking here, and I'll break your
        knave's pate.
DROMIO E. A man may break a word with you, sir, and words are but
        wind;   75
        Ay, and break it in your face, so he break it not behind.
DROMIO S. [*Within*] It seems thou wantest breaking. Out upon thee,
        hind!
DROMIO E. Here's too much 'Out upon thee.' I pray thee, let me in.
DROMIO S. [*Within*] Ay, when fowls have no feathers, and fish have no
        fin.
ANTIPHOLUS E. Well, I'll break in. Go borrow me a crow.   80
DROMIO E. A crow without feather, master? Mean you so?
        For a fish without a fin, there's a fowl without a feather.
        If a crow help us in, sirrah, we'll pluck a crow together.
ANTIPHOLUS E. Go, get thee gone. Fetch me an iron crow.

Balthasar persuades Antipholus to withdraw from the house and join him and Angelo at the Tiger for dinner. Antipholus resolves to give the chain to a girl at the Porpentine.

1 'A vulgar comment will be made of it' (whole class)

Balthasar's advice to Antipholus (lines 94–106) is to be patient, to refrain from trying to force the door with a crowbar, and to retire to the Tiger, returning later on his own to 'know the reason of this strange restraint'.

Imagine, as a crowd, you have witnessed Antipholus' attempt to enter his own house. Let the comments flow freely between yourselves about the reputation of Antipholus, and about the events you have heard about or witnessed.

2 Should there be an interval?

This is roughly the middle of the play. Should there be an interval in a play as short as this? If so, where should it come? Make your decision, then discuss with others to see if you agree.

3 From anger to good humour (in pairs)

Balthasar manages to turn Antipholus from anger at line 84 ('Fetch me an iron crow') to acceptance and even merriment at lines 107–8 ('You have prevailed. I will depart in quiet and in despite of mirth mean to be merry'). One person reads Balthasar's lines (lines 85–106) while the other (Antipholus) reacts to each point. Make his mood changes clear.

compass of suspect circle of suspicion
stirring passage bustling traffic
rout crowd

ungalled estimation perfect reputation
wench of excellent discourse a sweet-talking woman
desert deserving

BALTHASAR Have patience, sir. O, let it not be so.   85
          Herein you war against your reputation,
          And draw within the compass of suspect
          Th'unviolated honour of your wife.
          Once this: your long experience of her wisdom,
          Her sober virtue, years, and modesty,   90
          Plead on her part some cause to you unknown.
          And doubt not, sir, but she will well excuse
          Why at this time the doors are made against you.
          Be ruled by me. Depart in patience,
          And let us to the Tiger all to dinner,   95
          And about evening come yourself alone
          To know the reason of this strange restraint.
          If by strong hand you offer to break in
          Now in the stirring passage of the day,
          A vulgar comment will be made of it,   100
          And that supposèd by the common rout
          Against your yet ungallèd estimation
          That may with foul intrusion enter in
          And dwell upon your grave when you are dead.
          For slander lives upon succession,   105
          For ever housèd where it gets possession.
ANTIPHOLUS E. You have prevailed. I will depart in quiet,
          And in despite of mirth mean to be merry.
          I know a wench of excellent discourse,
          Pretty and witty; wild, and yet, too, gentle.   110
          There will we dine. This woman that I mean,
          My wife (but, I protest, without desert)
          Hath oftentimes upbraided me withal.
          To her will we to dinner. [To Angelo] Get you home
          And fetch the chain. By this, I know, 'tis made.   115
          Bring it, I pray you, to the Porpentine,
          For there's the house. That chain will I bestow –
          Be it for nothing but to spite my wife –
          Upon mine hostess there. Good sir, make haste.
          Since mine own doors refuse to entertain me,   120
          I'll knock elsewhere to see if they'll disdain me.
ANGELO I'll meet you at that place some hour hence.
ANTIPHOLUS E. Do so. – This jest shall cost me some expense.
                                                            Exeunt

Luciana, thinking Antipholus of Syracuse is the real husband, urges him to at least appear to be loyal to her sister Adriana, even if he has affairs with other women in Ephesus.

1 The shape of Luciana's speech

Write down the last word of each of the first eight lines of the speech. Once you have found the pattern, test whether it applies to the rest of the speech. Do the indentations at the beginning of some of the lines help you in any way to establish this pattern?

2 Luciana's speech (in pairs)

Write down what seem to you the three main couplets (two lines that make sense together) from Luciana's speech (lines 1–28). Either put them in order of priority, or arrange them in some way (e.g. by joining them with arrows, by giving them equal status) to show the relationship between them. Then compare what you have done with another pair. Do you agree with the advice Adriana gives?

3 Making a conversation (in pairs)

You can obtain fascinating effects when you re-organise two speeches as a conversation. Take one or two lines of Luciana's and follow them with one or two from Antipholus' (lines 29–52). Each person reads his or her own lines. Continue this alternating pattern of reading together. You can select any lines to make your joint reading as effective as you can. It need not be as long as fifty-two lines. Present your version to the rest of the class, and compare your 'conversation' with those of other pairs.

---

office duty
orator speaker
apparel dress
harbinger messenger
attaint corruption

at board when you sit down to eat
compact of credit made up of
 trust
vain false
hit of hit on

ACT 3   SCENE 2

Enter LUCIANA, with ANTIPHOLUS OF SYRACUSE

LUCIANA And may it be that you have quite forgot
    A husband's office? Shall, Antipholus,
Even in the spring of love thy love-springs rot?
    Shall love in building grow so ruinous?
If you did wed my sister for her wealth,   5
    Then for her wealth's sake use her with more kindness;
Or if you like elsewhere, do it by stealth.
    Muffle your false love with some show of blindness;
Let not my sister read it in your eye.
    Be not thy tongue thy own shame's orator.   10
Look sweet, speak fair, become disloyalty;
    Apparel vice like virtue's harbinger.
Bear a fair presence, though your heart be tainted;
    Teach sin the carriage of a holy saint.
Be secret-false; what need she be acquainted? –   15
    What simple thief brags of his own attaint?
'Tis double wrong to truant with your bed
    And let her read it in thy looks at board.
Shame hath a bastard fame, well managèd;
    Ill deeds is doubled with an evil word.   20
Alas, poor women, make us but believe,
    Being compact of credit, that you love us.
Though others have the arm, show us the sleeve.
    We in your motion turn, and you may move us.
Then, gentle brother, get you in again.   25
    Comfort my sister, cheer her, call her wife.
'Tis holy sport to be a little vain
    When the sweet breath of flattery conquers strife.
ANTIPHOLUS S. Sweet mistress, what your name is else I know not,
    Nor by what wonder you do hit of mine.   30
Less in your knowledge and your grace you show not
    Than our earth's wonder, more than earth divine.
Teach me, dear creature, how to think and speak.

Antipholus of Syracuse has fallen in love with Luciana and declares his passion for her. She thinks he is mad, and tries to deflect his love to Adriana, whom she thinks is his wife.

1 Writing a love poem

People who fall in love often write poems like the one below to their beloved.

> Come live with me and be my love,
> And we will all the pleasures prove
> That valleys, groves, hills and fields,
> Woods, or steepy mountain yields.
>
> And we will sit upon the rocks,
> Seeing the shepherds feed their flocks
> By shallow rivers, to whose falls
> Melodious birds sing madrigals.
>
> And I will make thee beds of roses,
> And a thousand fragrant posies,
> A cap of flowers, and a kirtle,
> Embroidered all with leaves of myrtle.

from Christopher Marlowe's *The Passionate Shepherd to his Love*

Either continue this poem in the same vein or write a 'reply' to it, using the same form, or write a modern version of it.

2 Advice to Luciana (in pairs)

Read lines 1–70 again. Imagine Luciana visits or writes to an agony aunt with her problem: her sister's husband seems to be in love with *her*! Work out your advice, and then either write the reply or improvise a scene in which the agony aunt – or uncle – delivers it. Luciana may well be unhappy with this advice and want to discuss the matter further.

---

conceit conception, ideas
mated confused, amazed

Lay open to my earthy gross conceit,
Smothered in errors, feeble, shallow, weak,   35
   The folded meaning of your words' deceit.
Against my soul's pure truth why labour you
   To make it wander in an unknown field?
Are you a god? Would you create me new?
   Transform me, then, and to your power I'll yield.   40
But if that I am I, then well I know
   Your weeping sister is no wife of mine,
Nor to her bed no homage do I owe.
   Far more, far more to you do I decline.
O, train me not, sweet mermaid, with thy note   45
   To drown me in thy sister's flood of tears.
Sing, siren, for thyself, and I will dote.
   Spread o'er the silver waves thy golden hairs
And as a bed I'll take thee, and there lie,
   And in that glorious supposition think   50
He gains by death that hath such means to die.
   Let love, being light, be drownèd if she sink.

LUCIANA What, are you mad, that you do reason so?
ANTIPHOLUS S. Not mad, but mated. How I do not know.
LUCIANA It is a fault that springeth from your eye.   55
ANTIPHOLUS S. For gazing on your beams, fair sun, being by.
LUCIANA Gaze where you should, and that will clear your sight.
ANTIPHOLUS S. As good to wink, sweet love, as look on night.
LUCIANA Why call you me 'love'? Call my sister so.
ANTIPHOLUS S. Thy sister's sister.
LUCIANA   That's my sister.
ANTIPHOLUS S.   No,   60
   It is thyself, mine own self's better part,
   Mine eye's clear eye, my dear heart's dearer heart,
   My food, my fortune, and my sweet hope's aim,
   My sole earth's heaven, and my heaven's claim.
LUCIANA All this my sister is, or else should be.   65
ANTIPHOLUS S. Call thyself sister, sweet, for I am thee.
   Thee will I love, and with thee lead my life.
   Thou hast no husband yet, nor I no wife.
   Give me thy hand.
LUCIANA   O soft, sir, hold you still.
   I'll fetch my sister to get her good will.   *Exit*   70

Dromio comes running to Antipholus for sanctuary. He is being chased by fat Nell, the kitchen wench, who wants to make love to him. Dromio begins to describe Nell's appearance with very unflattering comparisons.

1 An undesirable lover

Write about an encounter with someone who likes you but whom you find totally off-putting. Your description should be exaggerated and, if possible, comic. It could take the form of a dialogue – as in the details told by Dromio or Antipholus – or a monologue.

2 'What is she?' – illustrating Nell

From the information given in Dromio's description, draw a sketch of Nell. Compare your sketch with the illustration below.

rags clothes
tallow candle grease
swart black
ell forty-five inches (about 1.14 m)

Enter DROMIO OF SYRACUSE

ANTIPHOLUS S. Why, how now, Dromio. Where runnest thou so fast?

DROMIO S. Do you know me sir? Am I Dromio? Am I your man? Am I myself?

ANTIPHOLUS S. Thou art Dromio, thou art my man, thou art thyself.

DROMIO S. I am an ass, I am a woman's man, and besides myself.   75

ANTIPHOLUS S. What woman's man? And how besides thyself?

DROMIO S. Marry, sir, besides myself I am due to a woman, one that claims me, one that haunts me, one that will have me.

ANTIPHOLUS S. What claim lays she to thee?

DROMIO S. Marry, sir, such claim as you would lay to your horse; and   80
she would have me as a beast – not that, I being a beast, she would have me, but that she, being a very beastly creature, lays claim to me.

ANTIPHOLUS S. What is she?

DROMIO S. A very reverend body; ay, such a one as a man may not   85
speak of without he say 'sir-reverence'. I have but lean luck in the match, and yet is she a wondrous fat marriage.

ANTIPHOLUS S. How dost thou mean, a fat marriage?

DROMIO S. Marry, sir, she's the kitchen wench, and all grease; and I know not what use to put her to but to make a lamp of her and run   90
from her by her own light. I warrant her rags and the tallow in them will burn a Poland winter. If she lives till doomsday she'll burn a week longer than the whole world.

ANTIPHOLUS S. What complexion is she of?

DROMIO S. Swart like my shoe, but her face nothing like so clean kept.   95
For why? She sweats a man may go overshoes in the grime of it.

ANTIPHOLUS S. That's a fault that water will mend.

DROMIO S. No, sir, 'tis in grain. Noah's flood could not do it.

ANTIPHOLUS S. What's her name?

DROMIO S. Nell, sir. But her name and three quarters – that's an ell and   100
three quarters – will not measure her from hip to hip.

ANTIPHOLUS S. Then she bears some breadth?

DROMIO S. No longer from head to foot than from hip to hip. She is spherical, like a globe; I could find out countries in her.

ANTIPHOLUS S. In what part of her body stands Ireland.   105

DROMIO S. Marry, sir, in her buttocks. I found it out by the bogs.

ANTIPHOLUS S. Where Scotland?

*Prompted by Antipholus, Dromio continues to describe Nell in terms of
countries of the world. Antipholus decides they must leave Ephesus to get
away from the witchcraft that they have encountered there.*

1 'I could find out countries in her' (in pairs)

Lines 104–24 are some of the bawdiest (rudest) in the play.
Shakespeare plays upon the stereotypical characteristics of various
countries, punning upon their names and on other words associated
with them. Start at line 103 ('She is spherical, like a globe') and read
the dialogue in pairs. First, try it slowly, adding mime and/or
gestures. Then read it quickly (reversing roles) as a piece of repartee.

2 Write about a *man*!

Using an atlas, write a description of a male equivalent of Nell,
likening his appearance to various countries. Set it out as questions
and answers. You can either pun on the name of the country (e.g.
Chile), on the shape of it, or on some of its supposed characteristics.
Use different countries from those selected by Shakespeare.

3 Verse or prose?

Identify at which line the play moves from prose to verse. Suggest two
reasons why this might be so. Write out one or two of the verse
speeches in prose. Is anything lost by changing the verse to prose?

---

armed and reverted . . . heir a
reference to the civil war in France,
and a pun on 'hair'
armadoes of carracks armadas of
merchant ships
curtal dog a dog with a shortened
tail

turn i' the wheel tread a wheel to
turn a spit to roast meat
presently now, immediately
post hurry
abhor loathe, detest

DROMIO S. I found it by the barrenness, hard in the palm of the hand.

ANTIPHOLUS S. Where France?

DROMIO S. In her forehead, armed and reverted, making war against   110
her heir.

ANTIPHOLUS S. Where England?

DROMIO S. I looked for the chalky cliffs, but I could find no whiteness
in them. But I guess it stood in her chin, by the salt rheum that ran
between France and it.   115

ANTIPHOLUS S. Where Spain?

DROMIO S. Faith, I saw it not, but I felt it hot in her breath.

ANTIPHOLUS S. Where America, the Indies?

DROMIO S. O, sir, upon her nose, all o'er embellished with rubies,
carbuncles, sapphires, declining their rich aspect to the hot breath   120
of Spain, who sent whole armadoes of carracks to be ballast at her
nose.

ANTIPHOLUS S. Where stood Belgia, the Netherlands?

DROMIO S. O, sir, I did not look so low. To conclude, this drudge or
diviner laid claim to me, called me Dromio, swore I was assured to   125
her, told me what privy marks I had about me, as the mark of my
shoulder, the mole in my neck, the great wart on my left arm, that I,
amazed, ran from her as a witch.
  And I think if my breast had not been made of faith, and my
    heart of steel,
  She had transformed me to a curtal dog, and made me turn
    i'the wheel.   130

ANTIPHOLUS S. Go, hie thee presently. Post to the road.
  And if the wind blow any way from shore
  I will not harbour in this town tonight.
  If any bark put forth, come to the mart,
  Where I will walk till thou return to me.   135
  If everyone knows us, and we know none,
  'Tis time, I think, to trudge, pack, and be gone.

DROMIO S. As from a bear a man would run for life,
  So fly I from her that would be my wife.   *Exit*

ANTIPHOLUS S. There's none but witches do inhabit here,   140
  And therefore 'tis high time that I were hence.
  She that doth call me husband, even my soul
  Doth for a wife abhor. But her fair sister,
  Possessed with such a gentle sovereign grace,
  Of such enchanting presence and discourse,   145

Angelo the goldsmith gives Antipholus of Syracuse the chain intended for his twin brother. Antipholus accepts it, and goes off intending to catch the next ship out of Ephesus.

1 Mistaken identity yet again! (in groups of five or six)

Antipholus of Syracuse is again approached by someone who thinks they know him, but is mistaking him for the other Antipholus. This time it is Angelo, the goldsmith, with the chain he was to deliver to Antipholus of Ephesus at the Porpentine. To create the feeling of confusion and 'fairyland' wonderment, set Antipholus of Syracuse up in the middle of a space in the classroom or drama studio. As well as being approached by Angelo with the chain, create other characters who claim to know him from past encounters. Each can approach him from a different angle. Start the scene with Angelo's 'Master Antipholus' (line 148) and end it with 'I'll to the mart, and there for Dromio stay; if any ship put out, then straight away' (lines 168–9).

2 Conversation in a café (in pairs)

Imagine you are either Antipholus or Dromio of Syracuse. You are in a café at the port, and you give an account to someone you have just met of what has happened to you so far since arriving in Ephesus. As the conversation gains momentum, the listener asks further questions about why you are here, where you came from, what you hope to gain from your visit and why you now intend to leave!

3 'The mermaid's song' (line 148)

Mermaids were thought to lure sailors to their death by singing sweetly. Write a short story entitled 'The mermaid's song'.

---

bespoke ordered
vain foolish
shifts tricks

Pentecost Whitsun, fifty days after Easter
importuned troubled
Persia present-day Iran

Hath almost made me traitor to myself.
But lest myself be guilty to self-wrong,
I'll stop mine ears against the mermaid's song.

Enter ANGELO *with the chain*

ANGELO Master Antipholus.
ANTIPHOLUS S.   Ay, that's my name.
ANGELO I know it well, sir. Lo, here's the chain.   150
         I thought to have ta'en you at the Porpentine.
         The chain unfinished made me stay thus long.
ANTIPHOLUS S. What is your will that I shall do with this?
ANGELO What please yourself, sir. I have made it for you.
ANTIPHOLUS S. Made it for me, sir? I bespoke it not.   155
ANGELO Not once, nor twice, but twenty times you have.
         Go home with it, and please your wife withal,
         And soon at supper-time I'll visit you,
         And then receive my money for the chain.
ANTIPHOLUS S. I pray you, sir, receive the money now,   160
         For fear you ne'er see chain nor money more.
ANGELO You are a merry man, sir. Fare you well.   *Exit*
ANTIPHOLUS S. What I should think of this I cannot tell.
         But this I think, there's no man is so vain
         That would refuse so fair an offered chain.   165
         I see a man here needs not live by shifts,
         When in the streets he meets such golden gifts.
         I'll to the mart, and there for Dromio stay;
         If any ship put out, then straight away.   *Exit*

ACT 4   SCENE 1

Enter a SECOND MERCHANT, ANGELO *the goldsmith, and an* OFFICER

2 MERCHANT You know since Pentecost the sum is due,
         And since I have not much importuned you;
         Nor now I had not, but that I am bound
         To Persia, and want guilders for my voyage.

A merchant asks Angelo to repay a debt. Angelo replies he will pay with the money Antipholus owes. Antipholus of Ephesus enters, asking Angelo for the chain that was given to the other Antipholus. Confusion ensues.

1 Time chart

There are two clues in lines 7–11 of this scene as to the time and duration of the action of the play. Use these as the beginning of a time chart to show when the action of the play takes place. You will find other clues at 1.1.150, 1.2.11, 1.2.26, 3.2.158, 5.1.118 and elsewhere.

2 'A rope's end' (in pairs)

Talk together about what 'a rope's end' (line 16) tells you about Antipholus of Ephesus' character.

3 The flowing together of two conversations
(in groups of five)

The second merchant, Angelo and the officer are having one conversation (lines 1–14) while Antipholus and Dromio of Ephesus are having another (lines 15–21). Then Antipholus addresses Angelo. Map out, in an acting space, where the two groups of characters start from, and how and where they move. When Antipholus first addresses Angelo ('A man is well holp up that trusts to you'), what distance apart are they, and how loudly does he speak? Try lines 1–39 in various ways, until you feel you have the movements, the pace and the volume right.

---

present satisfaction immediate settlement of the debt
holp up helped

chargeful fashion costly craftsmanship
ducats gold coins
disburse pay

Therefore make present satisfaction,   5
Or I'll attach you by this officer.
ANGELO Even just the sum that I do owe to you
Is growing to me by Antipholus,
And in the instant that I met with you
He had of me a chain. At five o'clock   10
I shall receive the money for the same.
Pleaseth you walk with me down to his house,
I will discharge my bond, and thank you too.

Enter ANTIPHOLUS OF EPHESUS [*and*] DROMIO [OF EPHESUS] *from the*
Courtesan's

OFFICER That labour may you save. See where he comes.

ANTIPHOLUS E. While I go to the goldsmith's house, go thou   15
And buy a rope's end; that will I bestow
Among my wife and her confederates
For locking me out of my doors by day.
But soft, I see the goldsmith. Get thee gone.
Buy thou a rope, and bring it home to me.   20
DROMIO E. I buy a thousand pound a year, I buy a rope.   *Exit*
ANTIPHOLUS E. A man is well holp up that trusts to you.
I promisèd your presence and the chain,
But neither chain nor goldsmith came to me.
Belike you thought our love would last too long   25
If it were chained together, and therefore came not.
ANGELO Saving your merry humour, here's the note
How much your chain weighs to the utmost carat,
The fineness of the gold, and chargeful fashion,
Which doth amount to three odd ducats more   30
Than I stand debted to this gentleman.
I pray you see him presently discharged,
For he is bound to sea, and stays but for it.
ANTIPHOLUS E. I am not furnished with the present money;
Besides, I have some business in the town.   35
Good signior, take the stranger to my house,
And with you take the chain, and bid my wife
Disburse the sum on the receipt thereof.
Perchance I will be there as soon as you.

*Antipholus of Ephesus continues to assert that he has not received the chain.
Angelo and the merchant demand their payment. The merchant has Angelo
arrested, then Angelo has Antipholus arrested.*

1 The argument (in groups of four)

We know, of course, that Antipholus of Syracuse has the chain –
Angelo gave it to him in the previous scene. Nevertheless, an
argument develops from this misunderstanding. Cast and rehearse
lines 40–84, enjoying the confusion and the heated nature of the
exchange.

2 Who's who?

Here is a photograph from a production of the play in Dresden in
1950. Identify the characters, and the line at which this exchange
takes place. One of the four characters is missing. How would he be
dressed in this production?

dispatch deliver
**run this humour out of
breath** take this joke too far

at my suit at my request
fee officers were entitled to a fee for
such arrests

ANGELO Then you will bring the chain to her yourself.   40
ANTIPHOLUS E. No, bear it with you lest I come not time enough.
ANGELO Well, sir, I will. Have you the chain about you?
ANTIPHOLUS E. And if I have not, sir, I hope you have,
    Or else you may return without your money.
ANGELO Nay, come, I pray you, sir, give me the chain.   45
    Both wind and tide stays for this gentleman,
    And I, to blame, have held him here too long.
ANTIPHOLUS E. Good lord, you use this dalliance to excuse
    Your breach of promise to the Porpentine.
    I should have chid you for not bringing it,   50
    But like a shrew you first begin to brawl.
2 MERCHANT The hour steals on. I pray you, sir, dispatch.
ANGELO You hear how he importunes me. The chain!
ANTIPHOLUS E. Why, give it to my wife, and fetch your money.
ANGELO Come, come. You know I gave it you even now.   55
    Either send the chain, or send me by some token.
ANTIPHOLUS E. Fie, now you run this humour out of breath.
    Come, where's the chain? I pray you let me see it.
2 MERCHANT My business cannot brook this dalliance.
    Good sir, say whe'er you'll answer me or no.   60
    If not, I'll leave him to the officer.
ANTIPHOLUS E. I answer you? What should I answer you?
ANGELO The money that you owe me for the chain.
ANTIPHOLUS E. I owe you none till I receive the chain.
ANGELO You know I gave it you half an hour since.   65
ANTIPHOLUS E. You gave me none. You wrong me much to say so.
ANGELO You wrong me more, sir, in denying it.
    Consider how it stands upon my credit.
2 MERCHANT Well, officer, arrest him at my suit.
OFFICER   I do,
    And charge you in the Duke's name to obey me.   70
ANGELO This touches me in reputation.
    Either consent to pay this sum for me,
    Or I attach you by this officer.
ANTIPHOLUS E. Consent to pay thee that I never had?
    Arrest me, foolish fellow, if thou dar'st.   75
ANGELO Here is thy fee. Arrest him, officer.
    I would not spare my brother in this case
    If he should scorn me so apparently.

Dromio of Syracuse returns to tell the wrong Antipholus that a ship is waiting for them. Antipholus asks the puzzled Dromio for the rope, then sends him to Adriana for money to pay for his release from arrest.

1 Cross-examination (in groups of two or three)

Imagine that Antipholus of Ephesus is questioned by one or two police officers, who take down a statement from him. Enact the situation. Try to get information from Antipholus about the arrangement with Angelo and the whereabouts of the chain. The questions can go back to the attempt to get into the house in 3.1. Afterwards, write a statement for Antipholus that he must sign.

2 Further complications for Dromio of Syracuse (in pairs)

Read lines 85–113, and decide how Dromio and Antipholus should be played. Rehearse the lines, each of you taking Antipholus' part in different readings. Add movements and full expression to the lines, performing them in the way that seems best to you after your rehearsals.

3 Dromio's thoughts

Write a monologue, continuing Dromio's thoughts as he prepares to return to Adriana's house to face 'Dowsabel' (Nell/Luce). Try to capture the character of Dromio in your writing and include his reflections on his experiences so far in Ephesus. You can write in prose, or in Shakespearean blank verse. The finished piece can be performed, recorded or shown to others.

---

bark ship
fraughtage luggage
balsamum balm, ointment
aqua-vitae alcoholic spirits

waftage transportation across water
Dowsabel another name for Nell, meaning 'sweetheart'
compass embrace, win

OFFICER I do arrest you, sir. You hear the suit.

ANTIPHOLUS E. I do obey thee till I give thee bail.   80
        But, sirrah, you shall buy this sport as dear
        As all the metal in your shop will answer.

ANGELO Sir, sir, I shall have law in Ephesus,
        To your notorious shame, I doubt it not.

Enter DROMIO OF SYRACUSE *from the bay*

DROMIO S. Master, there's a bark of Epidamnum   85
        That stays but till her owner comes aboard,
        And then she bears away. Our fraughtage, sir,
        I have conveyed aboard, and I have bought
        The oil, the balsamum, and aqua-vitae.
        The ship is in her trim; the merry wind   90
        Blows fair from land. They stay for naught at all
        But for their owner, master, and yourself.

ANTIPHOLUS E. How now? A madman? Why, thou peevish sheep,
        What ship of Epidamnum stays for me?

DROMIO S. A ship you sent me to, to hire waftage.   95

ANTIPHOLUS E. Thou drunken slave, I sent thee for a rope,
        And told thee to what purpose, and what end.

DROMIO S. You sent me for a rope's end as soon.
        You sent me to the bay, sir, for a bark.

ANTIPHOLUS E. I will debate this matter at more leisure,   100
        And teach your ears to list me with more heed.
        To Adriana, villain, hie thee straight.
        Give her this key, and tell her in the desk
        That's covered o'er with Turkish tapestry
        There is a purse of ducats. Let her send it.   105
        Tell her I am arrested in the street,
        And that shall bail me. Hie thee, slave. Be gone.
        On, officer, to prison, till it come.

Exeunt [all but Dromio of Syracuse]

DROMIO S. To Adriana. That is where we dined,
        Where Dowsabel did claim me for her husband.   110
        She is too big, I hope, for me to compass.
        Thither I must, although against my will;
        For servants must their masters' minds fulfil.   *Exit*

Adriana cross-examines Luciana about Antipholus' approaches. She calls him all manner of names, then says that nevertheless she still loves him.

---

1 Are you serious? (in pairs)

How can you tell if someone is serious about you? Adriana quizzes her sister as to how Antipholus of Syracuse *looked* as he tried to woo her (chat her up). For fun, try to chat each other up in various ways, including 'or red or pale, or sad or merrily' (the first 'or' in each phrase means 'either'/'whether'). You can set these encounters in a café, at a bus stop, at a disco or wherever you think might be an appropriate or potentially funny location.

2 'He is deformèd, crooked, old and sere' (line 19)

Write a similarly vindictive description of someone who has jilted you, or of someone who has tried to chat you up but whom you don't fancy one bit! Write it in the same form as Adriana, using two pairs of rhyming couplets in ten-syllable lines. For further inspiration, see Dromio's description of the officer (lines 34–40).

Note the accent on the last syllable of 'deformèd'. This means that '-ed' should be pronounced as in 'head' or 'led'. So 'deformèd' would be pronounced with three syllables.

3 Comparing Adriana and Luciana

Compare this scene to 2.1, where we first meet Adriana and Luciana. Which of them would you most expect to:

a say one thing and mean another
b take a contemporary view of the rights of women
c be loyal
d be witty?

---

austerely truly, without deception
tilting jousting
sere dried-up

stigmatical in making deformed in appearance

ACT 4   SCENE 2

Enter ADRIANA and LUCIANA

ADRIANA Ah, Luciana, did he tempt thee so?
    Mightst thou perceive austerely in his eye
  That he did plead in earnest, yea or no?
    Looked he or red or pale, or sad or merrily?
  What observation mad'st thou in this case   5
  Of his heart's meteors tilting in his face?
LUCIANA First, he denied you had in him no right.
ADRIANA He meant he did me none, the more my spite.
LUCIANA Then swore he that he was a stranger here.
ADRIANA And true he swore, though yet forsworn he were.   10
LUCIANA Then pleaded I for you.
ADRIANA   And what said he?
LUCIANA That love I begged for you, he begged of me.
ADRIANA With what persuasion did he tempt thy love?
LUCIANA With words that in an honest suit might move.
  First he did praise my beauty, then my speech.   15
ADRIANA Didst speak him fair?
LUCIANA   Have patience, I beseech.
ADRIANA I cannot nor I will not hold me still.
  My tongue, though not my heart, shall have his will.
  He is deformèd, crooked, old, and sere;
  Ill-faced, worse-bodied, shapeless everywhere;   20
  Vicious, ungentle, foolish, blunt, unkind,
  Stigmatical in making, worse in mind.
LUCIANA Who would be jealous, then, of such a one?
  No evil lost is wailed when it is gone.
ADRIANA Ah, but I think him better than I say,   25
    And yet would herein others' eyes were worse.
  Far from her nest the lapwing cries away.
  My heart prays for him, though my tongue do curse.

Dromio of Syracuse asks for the money for Antipholus of Ephesus. He explains that Antipholus has been arrested, and describes the arresting officer. Adriana questions him about the reason for the arrest.

1 'What, is he arrested?' (in groups of four)

Imagine you are a husband or wife who receives news from a messenger that your partner has been arrested on some charge. You are at home with your brother/sister when you hear the news. Perhaps your partner was involved in something you did not know about? Perhaps you will not live together again. Take the roles of messenger, brother, sister, husband or wife. Improvise what happens.

2 Twelve ways of describing a policeman

Find the twelve different descriptions of the officer in lines 33–40. Then write a similarly rich description of a teacher, a politician, a bank manager or anyone else who can have power over you.

3 Time runs backwards! (in pairs)

'It was two ere I left him, and now the clock strikes one' (line 54)

This sense of the world turned upside-down often occurs in Shakespeare's plays, both in tragic and comic contexts. Here, in a humorous local sense, time turns back on itself when it meets an officer because it is 'in debt and theft' (line 61). First, perform small-scale versions of actions backwards, in time, like pouring a drink, walking a dog, etc. Then work out a series of scenes which move back in time. Finally, apply the 'backwards' principle to one scene or to a sequence of scenes in this play. What is the effect?

Tartar limbo a prison bordering hell
buff a hard-wearing, dullish material
countermands inhibits, constricts
counter against the game

draws dryfoot follows the trail
redemption ransom, to get him freed
band a pun on 'bond' (financial agreement) and 'neck band' (collar)

Enter DROMIO OF SYRACUSE

DROMIO S. Here, go – the desk, the purse, sweat now, make haste.
LUCIANA How hast thou lost thy breath?
DROMIO S.   By running fast.   30
ADRIANA Where is thy master, Dromio? Is he well?
DROMIO S. No. He's in Tartar limbo, worse than hell.
    A devil in an everlasting garment hath him,
    One whose hard heart is buttoned up with steel,
    A fiend, a fairy, pitiless and rough;   35
    A wolf, nay, worse, a fellow all in buff;
    A backfriend, a shoulder-clapper, one that countermands
    The passages of alleys, creeks, and narrow lands;
    A hound that runs counter, and yet draws dryfoot well;
    One that before the Judgement carries poor souls to hell.   40
ADRIANA Why, man, what is the matter?
DROMIO S. I do not know the matter, he is 'rested on the case.
ADRIANA What, is he arrested? Tell me at whose suit.
DROMIO S. I know not at whose suit he is arrested well;
    But is in a suit of buff which 'rested him, that can I tell.   45
    Will you send him, mistress, redemption, the money in his
        desk?
ADRIANA Go fetch it, sister.

                                             Exit Luciana

                 This I wonder at,
    That he unknown to me should be in debt.
    Tell me, was he arrested on a band?
DROMIO S. Not on a band, but on a stronger thing: 50
    A chain, a chain – do you not hear it ring?
ADRIANA What, the chain?
DROMIO S. No, no, the bell. 'Tis time that I were gone.
    It was two ere I left him, and now the clock strikes one.
ADRIANA The hours come back; that did I never hear.   55
DROMIO S. O yes, if any hour meet a sergeant 'a turns back for very
        fear.
ADRIANA As if time were in debt. How fondly dost thou reason!
DROMIO S. Time is a very bankrupt, and owes more than he's worth to
        season.

*Adriana sends Dromio of Syracuse off with the money. Meanwhile,
Antipholus of Syracuse is still waiting at the market for Dromio, wondering
why everyone treats him as a friend. Dromio arrives with the money.*

1 'Conceit, my comfort and my injury' (line 66)

'Conceit' means imagination, fancy. How can it be both a 'comfort'
and an 'injury'?

2 Yet more mistakes about identity
(in groups of six or seven)

Page 58 suggested recreating the confusion felt by Antipholus of
Syracuse by approaching him from various directions with reminders
of past encounters. Here, in his opening speech, he recounts some of
his experiences in Ephesus in which people 'salute me as if I were
their well-acquainted friend'.

Set up a series of cameos, or small scenes, to show what is
happening to Antipholus as he moves around Ephesus. For example:

- every one doth call me by my name
- some tender money to me
- some invite me
- some other give me thanks for kindnesses, etc.

Alternatively, use Antipholus as narrator, telling an audience what is
happening to him as characters mime the various encounters.

In both cases, how can you convey the impression that 'these are
but imaginary wiles'?

3 What might be happening? (in groups of three or four)

Devise a scene to show something of Antipholus' experience that is
not mentioned in the script, but which you can imagine might well
have happened to him.

---

conceit imagination
tender offer
wiles tricks
**what, have you got the picture of
old Adam new-apparelled?**
  Have you got rid of the officer? 'Old

Adam' was a name for wickedness,
the inhumanity that causes sin.
Dromio thinks that somehow
Antipholus has escaped from the
officer in the buff suit

Nay, he's a thief, too. Have you not heard men say
That time comes stealing on by night and day?   60
If 'a be in debt and theft, and a sergeant in the way,
Hath he not reason to turn back an hour in a day?

Enter LUCIANA

ADRIANA Go, Dromio, there's the money. Bear it straight,
 And bring thy master home immediately.
 Come, sister, I am pressed down with conceit –   65
 Conceit, my comfort and my injury.

Exeunt

ACT 4   SCENE 3

Enter ANTIPHOLUS OF SYRACUSE

ANTIPHOLUS S. There's not a man I meet but doth salute me
 As if I were their well-acquainted friend,
 And every one doth call me by my name.
 Some tender money to me, some invite me,
 Some other give me thanks for kindnesses.   5
 Some offer me commodities to buy.
 Even now a tailor called me in his shop
 And showed me silks that he had bought for me,
 And therewithal took measure of my body.
 Sure, these are but imaginary wiles,   10
 And Lapland sorcerers inhabit here.

Enter DROMIO OF SYRACUSE

DROMIO S. Master, here's the gold you sent me for. What, have you got
 the picture of old Adam new-apparelled?
ANTIPHOLUS S. What gold is this? What Adam dost thou mean?

71

*Dromio and Antipholus continue to joke about the officer. A woman –
the one that the other Antipholus was going to meet – invites them to
go with her. They suspect her to be a devil.*

1 Fantastic journeys

'we wander in illusions' (line 36)

There are many stories of masters and their servants wandering on adventures in strange and wonderful lands. The Spanish classic *Don Quixote* by Cervantes is one example. In film, *Crocodile Dundee, Being There* and Woody Allen's *The Purple Rose of Cairo* provide modern, and very different variations on the same idea of a main character exploring a new world.

As a long-term activity to accompany the reading of *The Comedy of Errors* create one or two characters who undertake a journey of exploration and (self-)discovery. Make the main character around your age, and travelling either:

a close to home, but in a previously unencountered area
b in another country
c in a wilderness
d in a different universe
e in a different period of time
f in his/her own past or future.

There are many other ideas you will be able to think of. You can use elements of this play or roam beyond it. Write your account of your travels in the form of a log in which you record your observations, feelings and experiences.

Your writing can be humorous or serious.

---

calf's skin the officer's leathers
prodigal wasteful (like the prodigal son in the Bible)
suits of durance hard-wearing prison garments, and a pun on 'lawsuits'
more exploits with his mace than a morris-pike more with his staff of office than a soldier would with a pike-staff

band bond
hoy small coasting vessel
angels gold coins
distract distracted, mad
habit clothes
ergo therefore
mend complete

DROMIO S. Not that Adam that kept the paradise, but that Adam that   15
    keeps the prison. He that goes in the calf's skin that was killed for
    the prodigal. He that came behind you, sir, like an evil angel, and
    bid you forsake your liberty.

ANTIPHOLUS S. I understand thee not.

DROMIO S. No? Why, 'tis a plain case: he that went like a bass viol in a   20
    case of leather; the man, sir, that when gentlemen are tired gives
    them a sob and rests them; he, sir, that takes pity on decayed men
    and gives them suits of durance; he that sets up his rest to do more
    exploits with his mace than a morris-pike.

ANTIPHOLUS S. What, thou meanest an officer?   25

DROMIO S. Ay, sir, the sergeant of the band; he that brings any man to
    answer it that breaks his band; one that thinks a man always going to
    bed, and says, 'God give you good rest.'

ANTIPHOLUS S. Well, sir, there rest in your foolery. Is there any ships
    puts forth tonight? May we be gone?   30

DROMIO S. Why, sir, I brought you word an hour since that the bark
    Expedition put forth tonight, and then were you hindered by the
    sergeant to tarry for the hoy Delay. Here are the angels that you sent
    for to deliver you.

ANTIPHOLUS S. The fellow is distract, and so am I,   35
    And here we wander in illusions,
    Some blessèd power deliver us from hence!

Enter a COURTESAN

COURTESAN Well met, well met, Master Antipholus.
    I see, sir, you have found the goldsmith now.
    Is that the chain you promised me today?   40

ANTIPHOLUS S. Satan, avoid! I charge thee, tempt me not.

DROMIO S. Master, is this Mistress Satan?

ANTIPHOLUS S. It is the devil.

DROMIO S. Nay, she is worse, she is the devil's dam; and here she
    comes in the habit of a light wench; and thereof comes that the   45
    wenches say, 'God damn me'; that's as much to say, 'God make me
    a light wench.' It is written they appear to men like angels of light.
    Light is an effect of fire, and fire will burn. Ergo, light wenches will
    burn. Come not near her.

COURTESAN Your man and you are marvellous merry, sir.   50
    Will you go with me? We'll mend our dinner here.

Antipholus and Dromio try to fend off the courtesan, but she claims her ring – or the chain. After they run off, she decides to visit Adriana to tell her about the stolen 'ring'.

1 The courtesan

Here is an engraving of the courtesan. Does she fit your interpretation of the words in the play?

2 What is she? (in pairs)

Some productions portray the courtesan as a prostitute, but on slim evidence. Read her lines (lines 38–88), alternating line by line until you find the tone that you think is right for her. Are her speeches heavy with sexual innuendo or not? Try the reading both ways.

3 'Now out of doubt Antipholus is mad . . .'
   (in groups of up to sixteen)

Sit in a circle and read, in turn, one line each of the courtesan's final speech. Then read it again, this time each person saying one word (the word they think most powerful, most important) only from each line. What atmosphere is built up by your chosen words?

4 A late arrival

Can you suggest reasons why a courtesan has been introduced into the action at this point – quite late in the play?

---

spoon-meat soft food
bespeak order
he must have . . . the devil a
  proverb
avaunt away with you

'fly pride' the peacock personifies
  pride; there is also a pun on sexual
  desire (pride = erect penis)
belike perhaps
ring a pun on her sexuality
  (ring = vagina)

DROMIO S. Master, if you do, expect spoon-meat, or bespeak a long
    spoon.
ANTIPHOLUS S. Why, Dromio?
DROMIO S. Marry, he must have a long spoon that must eat with the   55
    devil.
ANTIPHOLUS S. [*To Courtesan*] Avoid then, fiend. What tell'st thou me
      of supping?
    Thou art, as you are all, a sorceress.
    I conjure thee to leave me and be gone.
COURTESAN Give me the ring of mine you had at dinner,   60
    Or for my diamond the chain you promised,
    And I'll be gone, sir, and not trouble you.
DROMIO S. Some devils ask but the parings of one's nail,
    A rush, a hair, a drop of blood, a pin,
    A nut, a cherry stone.   65
    But she, more covetous, would have a chain.
    Master, be wise; and if you give it her,
    The devil will shake her chain, and fright us with it.
COURTESAN I pray you, sir, my ring, or else the chain.
    I hope you do not mean to cheat me so.   70
ANTIPHOLUS S. Avaunt, thou witch! Come, Dromio, let us go.
DROMIO S. 'Fly pride', says the peacock. Mistress, that you know.
                      Exeunt Antipholus and Dromio
COURTESAN Now out of doubt Antipholus is mad,
    Else would he never so demean himself.
    A ring he hath of mine worth forty ducats,   75
    And for the same he promised me a chain.
    Both one and other he denies me now.
    The reason that I gather he is mad,
    Besides this present instance of his rage,
    Is a mad tale he told today at dinner   80
    Of his own doors being shut against his entrance.
    Belike his wife, acquainted with his fits,
    On purpose shut the doors against his way.
    My way is now to hie home to his house,
    And tell his wife that, being lunatic,   85
    He rushed into my house and took perforce
    My ring away. This course I fittest choose,
    For forty ducats is too much to lose.   *Exit*

Dromio of Ephesus returns to his Antipholus with a short length of rope instead of the money Antipholus is expecting. He gets beaten for it.

---

1 Money for old rope: a children's story

Antipholus of Ephesus is expecting his Dromio to bring him the money from the desk 'That's covered o'er with Turkish tapestry' at his house. But all he arrives with is a length of rope that he was actually sent for earlier – the rope that Antipholus will 'bestow among my wife and her confederates for locking me out of my doors by day' (4.1.16–17). It was the *other* Dromio who was sent for the ducats, which he has since delivered to the other Antipholus.

Elements in the story like mistaken identity, the pairs of twins and, here, the exchange of a large sum of money for a piece of old rope, also appear in children's stories. Use these and any other elements in the play, and reframe them in a story for young children. You can illustrate your story and make it into a book for reading in local primary schools.

2 How to show the beatings (in pairs)

Antipholus is in a high state of anger in this scene, and lashes out at Dromio and at Dr Pinch. Rehearse these beatings in slow motion without actually touching each other. Then act out the scene quickly, adding words from the scene to accompany the 'blows'.

How can you make the audience laugh at these points?

3 Are these beatings acceptable on stage? (in fours)

The Antipholuses often beat the Dromios in this play and in this scene the blows are delivered particularly freely. One pair argues that this should not be allowed on a modern stage; the other pair argue that it is part of the comedy. Use as much evidence as you can recall to support your case. Then switch roles, and argue the other point of view.

---

ere before
attached under arrest
at the rate at that price

adversity trouble
nativity birth

ACT 4   SCENE 4

Enter ANTIPHOLUS OF EPHESUS *with the* JAILER

ANTIPHOLUS E. Fear me not, man. I will not break away.
　　　I'll give thee ere I leave thee so much money
　　　To warrant thee as I am 'rested for.
　　　My wife is in a wayward mood today,
　　　And will not lightly trust the messenger　　　　　　5
　　　That I should be attached in Ephesus.
　　　I tell you, 'twill sound harshly in her ears.

　　　Enter DROMIO OF EPHESUS, *with a rope's end*

　　　Here comes my man. I think he brings the money.
　　　How now, sir, have you that I sent you for?
DROMIO E. Here's that, I warrant you, will pay them all.　　　10
ANTIPHOLUS E. But where's the money?
DROMIO E. Why, sir, I gave the money for the rope.
ANTIPHOLUS E. Five hundred ducats, villain, for a rope?
DROMIO E. I'll serve you, sir, five hundred at the rate.
ANTIPHOLUS E. To what end did I bid thee hie thee home?　　　15
DROMIO E. To a rope's end, sir, and to that end am I returned.
ANTIPHOLUS E. And to that end, sir, I will welcome you.
　　　　　　　　　[He beats Dromio]
JAILER Good sir, be patient.
DROMIO E. Nay, 'tis for me to be patient. I am in adversity.
JAILER Good now, hold thy tongue.　　　20
DROMIO E. Nay, rather persuade him to hold his hands.
ANTIPHOLUS E. Thou whoreson, senseless villain.
DROMIO E. I would I were senseless, sir, that I might not feel your
　　　blows.
ANTIPHOLUS E. Thou art sensible in nothing but blows; and so is an　　　25
　　　ass.
DROMIO E. I am an ass indeed. You may prove it by my long ears. I have
　　　served him from the hour of my nativity to this instant, and have
　　　nothing at his hands for my service but blows. When I am cold, he

77

*Adriana and Luciana bring a schoolmaster, Dr Pinch, to try to cure
Antipholus of Ephesus of his apparent madness. Pinch also gets a beating
from the enraged Antipholus.*

1 Dr Pinch

Although Dr Pinch is described as a 'schoolmaster' he seems to be an
odd kind of teacher. A contemporary of Shakespeare described those,
like Dr Pinch, who claimed to cure all manner of diseases and
disorders, as being made up of:

'Tinkers, tooth-drawers, pedlers, ostlers, carters, porters, horse-
gelders & horse-leeches, ideots, apple-squires, broomemen,
bawds, witches, cuniurers, south-saiers and sow-gelders, roages,
rat-catchers, runagates & proctors of spitelehouses, with such other
lyke rotten and stincking weeds, which do in town & countrie,
without order, honestie or skil, daily abuse both phisick &
chirurgerie . . .'

(from William Clowes, *A Briefe and necessarie treatise touching the cure
of the disease called morbus gallicus*, 1585)

With the help of a dictionary, see if you can make sense of this
passage. Write a few remedies for ailments that some of these
characters (and Pinch himself) might have prescribed. Present them
as authentic late sixteenth-century documents by using ink, calli-
graphy, dyed papers and charred edges.

2 What would your Dr Pinch look like?

Using ideas from the script, design the costume you think Pinch
would wear in your production of *The Comedy of Errors*. How do your
ideas compare with the Royal Shakespeare Company's Dr Pinch on
page 80?

---

wont is used to do with
conjurer exorcist (because he can
  speak Latin, the language in which
  to exorcise spirits)

ecstasy frenzy
saffron orange-yellow
sooth true

heats me with beating; when I am warm, he cools me with beating; I   30
am waked with it when I sleep, raised with it when I sit, driven out of
doors with it when I go from home, welcomed home with it when I
return; nay, I bear it on my shoulders, as a beggar wont her brat, and
I think when he hath lamed me I shall beg with it from door to door.

> *Enter* ADRIANA, LUCIANA, *the* COURTESAN,
> *and a Schoolmaster called* PINCH

ANTIPHOLUS E. Come, go along; my wife is coming yonder.   35
DROMIO E. Mistress, *respice finem* – 'respect your end', or rather, to
    prophesy like the parrot, 'Beware the rope's end.'
ANTIPHOLUS E. Wilt thou still talk?

> *[He] beats Dromio*

COURTESAN How say you now? Is not your husband mad?
ADRIANA His incivility confirms no less.   40
    Good Doctor Pinch, you are a conjurer.
    Establish him in his true sense again,
    And I will please you what you will demand.
LUCIANA Alas, how fiery and how sharp he looks!
COURTESAN Mark how he trembles in his ecstasy.   45
PINCH Give me your hand, and let me feel your pulse.
ANTIPHOLUS E. There is my hand, and let it feel your ear.

> *[He strikes Pinch]*

PINCH I charge thee, Satan, housed within this man,
    To yield possession to my holy prayers.
    And to thy state of darkness hie thee straight.   50
    I conjure thee by all the saints in heaven.
ANTIPHOLUS E. Peace, doting wizard, peace. I am not mad.
ADRIANA O that thou wert not, poor distressèd soul!
ANTIPHOLUS E. You, minion, you, are these your customers?
    Did this companion with the saffron face   55
    Revel and feast it at my house today,
    Whilst upon me the guilty doors were shut,
    And I denied to enter in my house?
ADRIANA O, husband, God doth know you dined at home,
    Where would you had remained until this time,   60
    Free from these slanders and this open shame.
ANTIPHOLUS E. Dined at home? *[To Dromio]* Thou, villain, what sayst
    thou?
DROMIO E. Sir, sooth to say, you did not dine at home.

Antipholus, Dromio and Adriana accuse each other as they try to sort out the confusion. Antipholus gets even more angry as he assumes a plot. Adriana pleads that Antipholus be tied up.

1 Dr Pinch – a man of few words, but much action?

Dr Pinch has only eleven lines in the whole play. Collect them and work out how to say them. Is Pinch going to speak madly, wisely, gravely or in a combination of these and other ways?

2 Dealing with madness

Adriana has summoned Pinch to deal with Antipholus because she thinks he has gone mad. Find out from the library as much as you can about the symptoms, causes and treatments of 'madness', in Shakespeare's day and now. Have any advances been made?

Dr Pinch (Royal Shakespeare Company, 1983).

perdie par Dieu, by God
sans fable truly (literally, 'without story')
vestal vestal virgin, guardian of the kitchen fire

contraries extremes of humour
finds his vein discovers his master's frame of mind
suborned hired
dissembling deceiving

ANTIPHOLUS E. Were not my doors locked up, and I shut out?

DROMIO E. Perdie, your doors were locked, and you shut out.   65

ANTIPHOLUS E. And did not she herself revile me there?

DROMIO E. Sans fable, she herself reviled you there.

ANTIPHOLUS E. Did not her kitchen-maid rail, taunt, and scorn me?

DROMIO E. Certes she did. The kitchen vestal scorned you.

ANTIPHOLUS E. And did not I in rage depart from thence?   70

DROMIO E. In verity you did. My bones bears witness,
  That since have felt the vigour of his rage.

ADRIANA Is't good to soothe him in these contraries?

PINCH It is no shame. The fellow finds his vein,
  And yielding to him humours well his frenzy.   75

ANTIPHOLUS E. Thou has suborned the goldsmith to arrest me.

ADRIANA Alas, I sent you money to redeem you,
  By Dromio here, who came in haste for it.

DROMIO E. Money by me? Heart and good will you might,
  But surely, master, not a rag of money.   80

ANTIPHOLUS E. Went'st not thou to her for a purse of ducats?

ADRIANA He came to me, and I delivered it.

LUCIANA And I am witness with her that she did.

DROMIO E. God and the ropemaker bear me witness
  That I was sent for nothing but a rope.   85

PINCH Mistress, both man and master is possessed;
  I know it by their pale and deadly looks.
  They must be bound and laid in some dark room.

ANTIPHOLUS E. [*To Adriana*] Say, wherefore didst thou lock me forth
  today,
  [*To Dromio*] And why dost thou deny the bag of gold?   90

ADRIANA I did not, gentle husband, lock thee forth.

DROMIO E. And, gentle master, I received no gold.
  But I confess, sir, that we were locked out.

ADRIANA Dissembling villain, thou speak'st false in both.

ANTIPHOLUS E. Dissembling harlot, thou art false in all,   95
  And art confederate with a damnèd pack
  To make a loathsome abject scorn of me.
  But with these nails I'll pluck out these false eyes
  That would behold in me this shameful sport.

ADRIANA O, bind him, bind him, let him not come near me!   100

  Enter three or four and offer to bind him. He strives

Dromio is also tied up. Adriana pledges that she will pay the debt
Antipholus of Ephesus owes to Angelo, if the jailer will let him go.
Antipholus and Dromio are bundled off.

1 'Out on thee, villain! Wherefore dost thou mad me?'
(in groups of seven)

Make a tableau or snapshot to show the seven main characters on
stage in relation to each other at line 120. They are:

Adriana
Luciana
Pinch
courtesan
jailer
Antipholus
Dromio

Hold the 'freeze-frame' for thirty seconds. The rest of the class guess
who is playing each character. Discuss facial expression, posture, and
relative positions.

2 How do they get off-stage?

At the end of the thirty seconds, continue the action by moving into
the next four lines of the script (lines 120–3): from 'Out on thee
villain . . .' (Antipholus) to the departure of Antipholus, Dromio and
Pinch. Plan this departure carefully – will Pinch be chasing Antipholus and Dromio, or will it be the other way round? Or perhaps they
won't be running at all?

suffer let
suit legal position

PINCH More company! The fiend is strong within him.

LUCIANA Ay me, poor man, how pale and wan he looks.

ANTIPHOLUS E. What, will you murder me? Thou, jailer, thou,
    I am thy prisoner; wilt thou suffer them
    To make a rescue?

JAILER   Masters, let him go.   105
    He is my prisoner, and you shall not have him.

PINCH Go bind his man, for he is frantic too.

          [Dromio is bound]

ADRIANA What wilt thou do, thou peevish officer?
    Hast thou delight to see a wretched man
    Do outrage and displeasure to himself?   110

JAILER He is my prisoner. If I let him go,
    The debt he owes will be required of me.

ADRIANA I will discharge thee ere I go from thee.
    Bear me forthwith unto his creditor,
    And, knowing how the debt grows, I will pay it.   115
    Good Master Doctor, see him safe conveyed
    Home to my house. O most unhappy day!

ANTIPHOLUS E. O most unhappy strumpet!

DROMIO E. Master, I am here entered in bond for you.

ANTIPHOLUS E. Out on thee, villain! Wherefore dost thou mad me?   120

DROMIO E. Will you be bound for nothing? Be mad, good master; cry
  'the devil!'

LUCIANA God help, poor souls, how idly do they talk!

ADRIANA Go bear him hence. Sister, go you with me.
    Exeunt, [other than the] Jailer, Adriana, Luciana, and the Courtesan
    Say now, whose suit is he arrested at?   125

JAILER One Angelo, a goldsmith. Do you know him?

ADRIANA I know the man. What is the sum he owes?

JAILER Two hundred ducats.

ADRIANA   Say, how grows it due?

JAILER Due for a chain your husband had of him.

ADRIANA He did bespeak a chain for me, but had it not.   130

COURTESAN Whenas your husband all in rage today
    Came to my house and took away my ring,
    The ring I saw upon his finger now,
    Straight after did I meet him with a chain.

Antipholus of Syracuse and his Dromio appear. Luciana, Adriana and the jailer think that her husband and his Dromio have escaped, are mad, and are chasing them with swords. Antipholus determines to leave Ephesus.

1 What a surprise! (in groups of three or four)

'God, for thy mercy, they are loose again!' (line 138)

Adriana, Luciana and the jailer must be surprised to see Antipholus and Dromio on the loose. Only seconds earlier they seemed to be safely bound over. Now they are carrying rapiers. Improvise a scene in which there is an element of surprise – when two or three characters are surprised by the return or appearance of another.

This 'other' person could be:

- someone returning from a war or a long journey
- someone who had been almost totally forgotten
- someone returning from the dead
- or some other figure.

How can you introduce *real* surprise to the scene, in addition to the shock of seeing this person again?

2 'I see these witches are afraid of swords . . .' (in pairs)

It seems as though Antipholus and Dromio are always about to leave Ephesus on a ship, but somehow never quite get to the port. One of you take Antipholus' part and the other Dromio's. Read lines 141–51 in two ways: first, as if they do really intend to 'get their stuff aboard', and then as if they will most probably stay in Ephesus (which is what happens). Then try it a third way: with Antipholus eager to leave, and Dromio keen to stay. Which version do you prefer?

3 Act the whole scene

Scene 4 makes great theatre! Cast it and act it. How fast can you play it so that it is still intelligible to the audience?

ADRIANA It may be so, but I did never see it.   135
     Come, jailer, bring me where the goldsmith is.
     I long to know the truth hereof at large.

     Enter ANTIPHOLUS [OF SYRACUSE] *and* DROMIO [OF
          SYRACUSE], *with their rapiers drawn*

LUCIANA God, for thy mercy, they are loose again!
ADRIANA And come with naked swords. Let's call more help
     To have them bound again.
JAILER   Away, they'll kill us!   140
     Exeunt omnes [apart from Antipholus S. and Dromio S.],
              as fast as may be, frighted

ANTIPHOLUS S. I see these witches are afraid of swords.
DROMIO S. She that would be your wife now ran from you.
ANTIPHOLUS S. Come to the Centaur. Fetch our stuff from thence.
     I long that we were safe and sound aboard.
DROMIO S. Faith, stay here this night. They will surely do us no harm.   145
     You saw they speak us fair, give us gold. Methinks they are such a
     gentle nation that, but for the mountain of mad flesh that claims
     marriage of me, I could find it in my heart to stay here still, and turn
     witch.
ANTIPHOLUS S. I will not stay tonight for all the town;   150
     Therefore away, to get our stuff aboard.
                            Exeunt

Looking back at Act 4

1 A filmscript of a musical

Here is part of the filmscript for *The Boys from Syracuse*, a musical by Rodgers and Hart, loosely based on *The Comedy of Errors*. Try rewriting lines 1–34 of Act 4 Scene 4 with a view to filming it (or any section you like).

The filmscript consists of directions for the camera in the left column, and script for the actors in the right column. As you will see from this example, you can interpret the Shakespeare freely.

UNIVERSAL
The Boys From Syracuse
Part 2

---

1 **Part Title**

2 **Close view at hedge**
   LUCE and DROMIO #2 rise –
   PHYLLIS comes on – they
   talk –

   LUCE   I – I hope I wasn't too forward, milady.
   PHYLLIS   You've been too something. But I liked it. And I thought Dromio showed rare discrimination. You're very lucky to have

3 **Close up LUCE & DROMIO**
   Standing

   PHYLLIS   *(Off scene)* a husband with such bright ideas.
   LUCE   Oh, he has ideas – but not about dancing.
   ADRIANA   *(Off scene)* Dromio!

4 **Close view at hedge**
   Three standing – ADRIANA
   comes on – talks

   DROMIO   Yes ma'am.
   ADRIANA   I thought I sent you after my husband.
   DROMIO   I did go look for him.
   ADRIANA   Well, where is he?
   DROMIO   He's at the Duke's Palace.
   ADRIANA   That's what *he* says.
   DROMIO   If that's what he says, that's where he is.
   ADRIANA   Dromio!

5 **Close up ADRIANA**
   Talking – angry – exits

   ADRIANA   You're two of a kind - you and Antipholus! Go and get him! I promise you the lashing of your life if he isn't home in time for dinner – sober!

6 **Close up of LUCE & DROMIO**
   Looking off – he talks –
   exits

   DROMIO   Madam, I'm a slave – not a magician.
   LUCE   Nomflirty-flirty or Mama hurty-hurty.
   DROMIO   Ooooh!

2 How is it going to end? (in groups of three or four)

Now that you have come to the end of Act 4, how do you think the play is going to end? Discuss your predictions of the ending. You need to take into account all of the following, as well as other elements that you consider to be important to the outcome of the action:

- the fate of Egeon
- Antipholus of Syracuse's desire to escape from Ephesus
- the master/slave relationships
- the 'madness' of Antipholus of Ephesus, and the fact that he and his Dromio are locked up
- the problem with the chain
- the position of Adriana, and her relationship with her sister
- the courtesan.

Once you have decided how you think the play will end, produce a short mime as a summary of the last act showing what you think will happen. One of these mimes occurs in *Hamlet*, another Shakespeare play, and is called a 'dumb show'.

3 Who's who?

When you have made your predictions and acted the mime, look at the photograph below from the last act of the 1983 RSC production. Guess who the characters are, and what is happening at this moment.

How does this version compare to yours?

One of the characters shown has not so far appeared in the play, but will play a significant part in Act 5.

Angelo and the merchant encounter Antipholus of Syracuse and Dromio on the street. Antipholus is wearing the chain. Antipholus and the merchant argue, then fight.

1 The chain again

How does Antipholus of Syracuse happen to be wearing the chain? Trace its whereabouts from its first mention in 3.1 up to now. Imagine, as an officer, you had to give a verbal report at a magistrates' hearing of its history. Make notes of where it is mentioned in the play, and whose hands it passes through.

2 Angelo's mood – and Antipholus' response (in pairs)

How is Angelo going to say lines 10–22? Is he fearful of Antipholus and of the merchant, or is he angry? Read the speech in these and various other ways, with Antipholus reacting according to the approach that Angelo takes towards him.

3 Build up to a fight (in pairs)

Fights do not often come out of the blue – there is usually a build-up through words. Create a short scene from the moment two characters sense an antagonism between them. It could simply start with an exchange of glances, through verbal exchanges to the moment when the argument moves into physical fighting. Freeze at the moment before the fight actually begins. Talk together about the differences between your improvisation and lines 1–32.

---

his word might . . . wealth his word would be enough to secure a loan on all my wealth

forswore swore
circumstance argument
impeach accuse

ACT 5   SCENE 1

Enter the SECOND MERCHANT *and* ANGELO *the goldsmith*

ANGELO I am sorry, sir, that I have hindered you,
       But I protest he had the chain of me,
       Though most dishonestly he doth deny it.
2 MERCHANT How is the man esteemed here in the city?
ANGELO Of very reverend reputation, sir;   5
       Of credit infinite, highly beloved,
       Second to none that lives here in the city.
       His word might bear my wealth at any time.
2 MERCHANT Speak softly. Yonder, as I think, he walks.

Enter ANTIPHOLUS [OF SYRACUSE] *and* DROMIO
      [OF SYRACUSE] *again*

ANGELO 'Tis so; and that self chain about his neck   10
       Which he forswore most monstrously to have.
       Good sir, draw near to me; I'll speak to him.
       Signior Antipholus, I wonder much
       That you would put me to this shame and trouble,
       And not without some scandal to yourself,   15
       With circumstance and oaths so to deny
       This chain, which now you wear so openly.
       Beside the charge, the shame, imprisonment,
       You have done wrong to this my honest friend,
       Who, but for staying on our controversy,   20
       Had hoisted sail and put to sea today.
       This chain you had of me. Can you deny it?
ANTIPHOLUS S. I think I had. I never did deny it.
2 MERCHANT Yes, that you did, sir, and forswore it, too.
ANTIPHOLUS S. Who heard me to deny it or forswear it?   25
2 MERCHANT These ears of mine, thou know'st, did hear thee.
       Fie on thee, wretch. 'Tis pity that thou liv'st
       To walk where any honest men resort.
ANTIPHOLUS S. Thou art a villain to impeach me thus.
       I'll prove mine honour and mine honesty
       Against thee presently, if thou dar'st stand.   30
2 MERCHANT I dare, and do defy thee for a villain.
                They draw

Antipholus and Dromio take refuge in the priory. Aemilia, the Abbess,
appears and questions Adriana about the behaviour and moods of
Antipholus. She wonders if Adriana has been too lenient with her husband.

1 Reaching sanctuary (in small groups)

'This is some priory. In, or we are spoiled.' (line 37)

The priory acts as a sanctuary, a safe place, for Antipholus and Dromio of Syracuse. Once inside, they cannot be arrested by their assailants.

Think of as many games as you can that have an element of sanctuary in them – games like 'off-ground touch' where you can't be caught if you find somewhere to perch above ground level.

Explore the idea of sanctuary more fully. What kinds of sanctuary exist now? Discuss reasons for seeking sanctuary. Devise a short play or story in which someone being pursued takes refuge in a sanctuary.

2 The anatomy of melancholy (in pairs)

'This week he hath been heavy, sour, sad . . .' (line 45)

The Abbess makes a number of suggestions to explain why Antipholus is 'heavy, sour, sad' (lines 49–54). Make a list of different kinds of bad mood (melancholy). Arrange the different moods into groups that have something in common. Then suggest reasons for moods like this. Do different reasons set off different moods? Is there any way to get out of these moods? Share your observations with another pair.

Either create a guide to melancholy which sets out the different moods, possible reasons for them and how to get out of them (with illustrations if you like). Such a book was published in 1621 by Robert Burton, *The Anatomy of Melancholy*. It was one of the first books to deal with what we now call psychology.

Or present a series of cameos, or short scenes, depicting various kinds of mood.

---

take (line 36) get into
possession madness
haply perhaps

copy of our conference theme of
our arguments

Enter ADRIANA, LUCIANA, *the* COURTESAN, *and others*

ADRIANA Hold, hurt him not, for God's sake; he is mad.
　　　　　Some get within him, take his sword away.
　　　　　Bind Dromio too, and bear them to my house.　　　　35
DROMIO S. Run, master, run! For God's sake take a house.
　　　　　This is some priory. In, or we are spoiled.
　　　　　Exeunt [Antipholus of Syracuse and Dromio of Syracuse] to the priory

Enter [ÆMILIA, the] Lady Abbess

ABBESS Be quiet, people. Wherefore throng you hither?
ADRIANA To fetch my poor distracted husband hence.
　　　　　Let us come in, that we may bind him fast　　　　40
　　　　　And bear him home for his recovery.
ANGELO I knew he was not in his perfect wits.
2 MERCHANT I am sorry now that I did draw on him.
ABBESS How long hath this possession held the man?
ADRIANA This week he hath been heavy, sour, sad,　　　　45
　　　　　And much, much different from the man he was.
　　　　　But till this afternoon his passion
　　　　　Ne'er brake into extremity of rage.
ABBESS Hath he not lost much wealth by wrack of sea?
　　　　　Buried some dear friend? Hath not else his eye　　　　50
　　　　　Strayed his affection in unlawful love –
　　　　　A sin prevailing much in youthful men,
　　　　　Who give their eyes the liberty of gazing?
　　　　　Which of these sorrows is he subject to?
ADRIANA To none of these except it be the last,　　　　55
　　　　　Namely some love that drew him oft from home.
ABBESS You should for that have reprehended him.
ADRIANA Why, so I did.
ABBESS　　　　　　　　Ay, but not rough enough.
ADRIANA As roughly as my modesty would let me.
ABBESS Haply in private.
ADRIANA　　　　　　　　And in assemblies, too.　　　　60
ABBESS Ay, but not enough.
ADRIANA It was the copy of our conference.
　　　　　In bed he slept not for my urging it;
　　　　　At board he fed not for my urging it.
　　　　　Alone, it was the subject of my theme;　　　　65
　　　　　In company I often glanced at it.
　　　　　Still did I tell him it was vile and bad.

Aemilia rebukes Adriana for driving Antipholus to madness with her jealousy, but Luciana urges Adriana to fight back. Adriana tries to extract Antipholus from the priory, but Aemilia refuses to let him go.

1 Aemilia's explanation of Antipholus' madness (in pairs)

With your partner, read alternate lines (lines 68–86). Take the lines slowly. Read them again in the same way. Now write down what seem to you to be the most important phrases in the speech that explain the reasons for Antipholus' 'madness'. Compare your choices with those of other pairs.

2 'Why bear you these rebukes, and answer not?' (in pairs)

Work out a dialogue between Luciana and Adriana in which they discuss the accusation of jealousy that the Abbess makes. Rehearse this, and then insert it between lines 89 and 90 (after 'Why bear you these rebukes . . .'). Then show your scene, framing your dialogue with Luciana's beginning 'She never reprehended him but mildly . . .' and with Adriana's 'She did betray me to my own reproof. Good people, enter, and lay hold on him.'

3 Adriana's case

Write a speech of about twenty lines in which Adriana uses all her powers to persuade the Abbess that she should gain access to her 'husband'. You can write this in prose, or use blank verse.

---

kinsman relation
distemperatures ailments
betray trick

assaying trying
formal normal
parcel part

ABBESS   And thereof came it that the man was mad.
            The venom clamours of a jealous woman
            Poisons more deadly than a mad dog's tooth.   70
            It seems his sleeps were hindered by thy railing,
            And thereof comes it that his head is light.
            Thou sayst his meat was sauced with thy upbraidings;
            Unquiet meals make ill digestions.
            Thereof the raging fire of fever bred;   75
            And what's a fever but a fit of madness?
            Thou sayst his sports were hindered by thy brawls;
            Sweet recreation barred, what doth ensue
            But moody and dull melancholy,
            Kinsman to grim and comfortless despair,   80
            And at her heels a huge infectious troop
            Of pale distemperatures and foes to life?
            In food, in sport, and life-preserving rest
            To be disturbed would mad or man or beast.
            The consequence is, then, thy jealous fits   85
            Hath scared thy husband from the use of wits.
LUCIANA   She never reprehended him but mildly,
            When he demeaned himself rough, rude, and wildly.
            [To Adriana] Why bear you these rebukes, and answer not?
ADRIANA   She did betray me to my own reproof.   90
            Good people, enter, and lay hold on him.
ABBESS   No, not a creature enters in my house.
ADRIANA   Then let your servants bring my husband forth.
ABBESS   Neither. He took this place for sanctuary,
            And it shall privilege him from your hands   95
            Till I have brought him to his wits again,
            Or lose my labour in assaying it.
ADRIANA   I will attend my husband, be his nurse,
            Diet his sickness, for it is my office,
            And will have no attorney but myself.   100
            And therefore let me have him home with me.
ABBESS   Be patient, for I will not let him stir
            Till I have used the approvèd means I have,
            With wholesome syrups, drugs, and holy prayers,
            To make of him a formal man again.   105
            It is a branch and parcel of mine oath,
            A charitable duty of my order.
            Therefore depart, and leave him here with me.

Adriana pleads for the return of her husband to the Duke, who is on his way to oversee the execution of Egeon.

---

1 The end of the road for Egeon?

In the first scene of the play, Egeon tells the story (lines 36–139) of how he came to Ephesus, and was sentenced to death by the Duke unless a ransom of a thousand marks was paid. Talk together about your reactions to the re-appearance of Egeon at this stage in the play. Some points to consider are:

a if this is a comedy, why is an execution about to take place?
b why do Egeon and the Duke enter at this point?
c what is going to happen?

2 The entry of the Duke (in groups of twelve)

Should this be a sombre entry, restoring the atmosphere of the first scene? Should it be formal and ceremonial, or human-scaled and informal? If there is to be a large change of mood, how is it to be brought about? Act out lines 128–32, showing your version of the entry and its effect.

3 Find the best way for Adriana to tell her story
(in groups of three or four)

Try showing lines 136–60 in various ways:

a told with exaggerated gestures by Adriana
b told by Adriana with Luciana miming the actions
c told by Adriana, but with the rest of the actors miming the action
d told simply by Adriana, on her knees.

Which works best?

---

beseem fit
tender value

important letters urgent
recommendations
take order for make arrangements
for

ADRIANA I will not hence and leave my husband here.
    And ill it doth beseem your holiness   110
    To separate the husband and the wife.
ABBESS Be quiet, and depart. Thou shalt not have him.   *[Exit]*
LUCIANA *[To Adriana]* Complain unto the Duke of this indignity.
ADRIANA Come, go. I will fall prostrate at his feet,
    And never rise until my tears and prayers   115
    Have won his grace to come in person hither
    And take perforce my husband from the Abbess.
2 MERCHANT By this, I think, the dial points at five.
    Anon, I'm sure, the Duke himself in person
    Comes this way to the melancholy vale,   120
    The place of death and sorry execution
    Behind the ditches of the abbey here.
ANGELO Upon what cause?
2 MERCHANT To see a reverend Syracusian merchant,
    Who put unluckily into this bay   125
    Against the laws and statutes of this town,
    Beheaded publicly for his offence.
ANGELO See where they come. We will behold his death.
LUCIANA Kneel to the Duke before he pass the abbey.

*Enter [*SOLINUS,*] the Duke of Ephesus, and [*EGEON,*] the Merchant of*
  Syracuse, barehead, with the HEADSMAN, *and other officers*

DUKE Yet once again proclaim it publicly.   130
    If any friend will pay the sum for him,
    He shall not die, so much we tender him.
ADRIANA Justice, most sacred Duke, against the Abbess!
DUKE She is a virtuous and a reverend lady.
    It cannot be that she hath done thee wrong.   135
ADRIANA May it please your grace, Antipholus my husband,
    Who I made lord of me and all I had
    At your important letters – this ill day
    A most outrageous fit of madness took him,
    That desperately he hurried through the street,   140
    With him his bondman all as mad as he,
    Doing displeasure to the citizens
    By rushing in their houses, bearing thence
    Rings, jewels, anything his rage did like.
    Once did I get him bound, and sent him home   145
    Whilst to take order for the wrongs I went,

The Duke sends for the Abbess so that he can solve the problem.
A messenger arrives to tell Adriana that her real husband and Dromio
have escaped, and are creating havoc.

1 Adriana's plea

Adriana is pleading to the Duke to use his power to release her husband from the abbey. Does her expression in this rehearsal photograph from the RSC 1990 production match the way you would have her play this speech?

2 Madness 'broke loose' (in groups of five to eight)

Act out the messenger's story (lines 169–77) in mime, showing every detail he describes.

wot know	**shift** make off
ireful angry	**a-row** one after another
	puddled mire filthy water

That here and there his fury had committed.
Anon, I wot not by what strong escape,
He broke from those that had the guard of him,
And with his mad attendant and himself,   150
Each one with ireful passion, with drawn swords
Met us again, and, madly bent on us,
Chased us away; till, raising of more aid,
We came again to bind them. Then they fled
Into this abbey, whither we pursued them;   155
And here the Abbess shuts the gates on us,
And will not suffer us to fetch him out,
Nor send him forth that we may bear him hence.
Therefore, most gracious Duke, with thy command
Let him be brought forth, and borne hence for help.   160

DUKE Long since thy husband served me in my wars,
And I to thee engaged a prince's word,
When thou didst make him master of thy bed,
To do him all the grace and good I could.
Go, some of you, knock at the abbey gate,   165
And bid the Lady Abbess come to me.
I will determine this before I stir.

Enter a MESSENGER

MESSENGER O mistress, mistress, shift and save yourself!
My master and his man are both broke loose,
Beaten the maids a-row, and bound the Doctor,   170
Whose beard they have singed off with brands of fire,
And ever as it blazed they threw on him
Great pails of puddled mire to quench the hair.
My master preaches patience to him, and the while
His man with scissors nicks him like a fool;   175
And sure, unless you send some present help,
Between them they will kill the conjurer.

ADRIANA Peace, fool; thy master and his man are here,
And that is false thou dost report to us.

MESSENGER Mistress, upon my life I tell you true.   180
I have not breathed almost since I did see it.
He cries for you, and vows, if he can take you,
To scorch your face and to disfigure you.
        Cry within
Hark, hark, I hear him, mistress. Fly, be gone!

Antipholus of Ephesus and his Dromio enter, amazing
Adriana who thinks he is in the abbey. Egeon recognises his son Antipholus.
Antipholus pleads to the Duke for justice.

---

1 'Ay me, it is my husband'

Act out Adriana's short speech (lines 186–9) in various ways. Try extremes of surprise, shock, delight, bewilderment. Will Adriana say these lines out loud, addressed to the whole group, to a particular character, or quietly, to herself? Which way do you think is most appropriate?

2 A barrister's speech

Imagine that, like a barrister, you are arguing the case for Antipholus of Ephesus in court. Prepare your case, finding evidence to support your argument. You can quote from the play (the source of your 'evidence') as well as make points about Antipholus' character and background, going back as far as the shipwreck thirty-three years ago (see line 400). Write the speech that you will give in court in the trial of Antipholus of Ephesus.

3 A court scene (whole class)

A court scene to pass judgement on Antipholus (and any other character) needs careful planning and preparation. The Duke can sit as judge, and a jury can be appointed to recommend a verdict to the judge. Barristers arguing for and against the cause of Antipholus can speak, and witnesses be called to give their evidence. Any of the characters can be called by either of the barristers, but all the evidence offered must remain true to the play itself.

4 'I see my son Antipholus, and Dromio'

Continue this aside (line 196) in writing, with Egeon wondering to himself how his son and his servant could be here, in Ephesus.

---

halberds spears with axe-heads
bestrid stood over
dote lose my wits
in the strength and height of
  injury in the most hurtful way
  possible

discover reveal
perjured sworn falsely
packed with in league with

DUKE Come, stand by me. Fear nothing. Guard with halberds!   185
ADRIANA Ay me, it is my husband. Witness you
       That he is borne about invisible.
       Even now we housed him in the abbey here,
       And now he's there, past thought of human reason.

Enter ANTIPHOLUS OF EPHESUS *and* DROMIO OF EPHESUS

ANTIPHOLUS E. Justice, most gracious Duke, O grant me justice,   190
       Even for the service that long since I did thee
       When I bestrid thee in the wars, and took
       Deep scars to save thy life. Even for the blood
       That then I lost for thee, now grant me justice.
EGEON [*Aside*] Unless the fear of death doth make me dote,   195
       I see my son Antipholus, and Dromio.
ANTIPHOLUS E. Justice, sweet prince, against that woman there,
       She whom thou gav'st to me to be my wife;
       That hath abusèd and dishonoured me
       Even in the strength and height of injury.   200
       Beyond imagination is the wrong
       That she this day hath shameless thrown on me.
DUKE Discover how, and thou shalt find me just.
ANTIPHOLUS E. This day, great Duke, she shut the doors upon me
       While she with harlots feasted in my house.   205
DUKE A grievous fault. Say, woman, didst thou so?
ADRIANA No, my good lord. Myself, he, and my sister
       Today did dine together. So befall my soul,
       As this is false he burdens me withal.
LUCIANA Ne'er may I look on day nor sleep on night   210
       But she tells to your highness simple truth.
ANGELO [*Aside*] O perjured woman! They are both forsworn;
       In this the madman justly chargeth them.
ANTIPHOLUS E. My liege, I am advisèd what I say,
       Neither disturbed with the effect of wine   215
       Nor heady-rash provoked with raging ire,
       Albeit my wrongs might make one wiser mad.
       This woman locked me out this day from dinner.
       That goldsmith there, were he not packed with her,
       Could witness it, for he was with me then,   220
       Who parted with me to go fetch a chain,

Antipholus of Ephesus tells his story to the Duke,
explaining that he never received the chain and was arrested, assailed by
Dr Pinch then locked up at home.

1 Antipholus' story (in groups of four to eight)

Lines 218–54 are a dramatic reminder of Antipholus' view of what
has happened in the play. **Either** act them out, showing every
episode, **or** prepare a radio broadcast of the lines.

At some points you can use a single voice. At others have two or
more voices speaking together. You may decide to change voices
every sentence. Put as much variety and drama as possible into your
radio broadcast of Antipholus' story.

Then get into groups of three or four, and decide on the best
strategy for the speech, combining your best ideas. Now try out your
plan. Rehearse it until you are satisfied, then present your performance to the rest of the class.

2 'A mere anatomy, a mountebank . . .'

Here is your chance to write an exaggerated and comic extension to
Antipholus' description of Pinch, full of imaginatively conceived
insults.

Copy lines 237–42 ('Along with them they brought one Pinch . . .'
to 'a living dead man'.) and continue from there. Who can compose
the most outrageously funny lines?

---

perjured lying
peasant servant
anatomy skeleton

mountebank quack, poseur
pernicious swift
in sunder apart

Promising to bring it to the Porpentine,
Where Balthasar and I did dine together.
Our dinner done, and he not coming thither,
I went to seek him. In the street I met him,   225
And in his company that gentleman.
There did this perjured goldsmith swear me down
That I this day of him received the chain,
Which, God he knows, I saw not. For the which
He did arrest me with an officer.   230
I did obey, and sent my peasant home
For certain ducats. He with none returned.
Then fairly I bespoke the officer
To go in person with me to my house.
By the way we met   235
My wife, her sister, and a rabble more
Of vile confederates. Along with them
They brought one Pinch, a hungry, lean-faced villain,
A mere anatomy, a mountebank,
A threadbare juggler and a fortune-teller,   240
A needy, hollow-eyed, sharp-looking wretch,
A living dead man. This pernicious slave,
Forsooth, took on him as a conjurer,
And gazing in mine eyes, feeling my pulse
And with no face, as 'twere, outfacing me,   245
Cries out I was possessed. Then all together
They fell upon me, bound me, bore me thence,
And in a dark and dankish vault at home
There left me and my man, both bound together,
Till, gnawing with my teeth my bonds in sunder,   250
I gained my freedom, and immediately
Ran hither to your grace, whom I beseech
To give me ample satisfaction
From these deep shames and great indignities.
ANGELO My lord, in truth, thus far I witness with him: 255
        That he dined not at home, but was locked out.
DUKE But had he such a chain of thee, or no?
ANGELO He had, my lord, and when he ran in here
        These people saw the chain about his neck.

Antipholus of Ephesus denies he was ever in the abbey.
The Duke is baffled by the contradictions. Egeon appeals to his son
Antipholus and Dromio, but neither recognises him.

1 All change! (in groups of four to six)

'I think you all have drunk of Circe's cup' (line 271)

In the ancient Greek story of Odysseus and his adventures, the crew of Odysseus' ship are tempted to drink a potion on Circe's island and are transformed into beasts. Set up a situation in which the crew find themselves on a strange island, are persuaded to drink such a potion, and are transformed in some way. The transformation need not be from human to animal, but could be a change into some other kind of person, or to develop a different aspect of personality. The changes need not all be obvious, but can be shown in subtle and understated ways. Then enter Odysseus, who attempts to communicate with his crew and to free them from this curse.

2 'I never saw you in my life till now' (line 297) (in pairs)

Someone recognises you, but you 'never saw them in your life till now'. Develop a scene in which such an encounter takes place, and decide how far you will take it until you resolve it in some way. How can you resolve it?

3 Choose a single line

Choose a single line from the opposite page that best sums up the play as a whole. Compare notes with others to see if you agree.

---

impeach accusation
Circe's cup the sorceress Circe, in Greek myth, changed men into pigs
mated stupefied

vouchsafe permit
bondman fellow prisoner (and pun on servant)

2 MERCHANT [*To Antipholus*] Besides, I will be sworn these ears of
        mine   260
        Heard you confess you had the chain of him
        After you first forswore it on the mart,
        And thereupon I drew my sword on you;
        And then you fled into this abbey here,
        From whence I think you are come by miracle.   265
ANTIPHOLUS E. I never came within these abbey walls,
        Nor ever didst thou draw thy sword on me.
        I never saw the chain, so help me heaven,
        And this is false you burden me withal.
DUKE Why, what an intricate impeach is this!   270
        I think you all have drunk of Circe's cup.
        If here you housed him, here he would have been.
        If he were mad, he would not plead so coldly.
        [*To Adriana*] You say he dined at home. The goldsmith here
        Denies that saying. [*To Dromio*] Sirrah, what say you?   275
DROMIO E. Sir, he dined with her there, at the Porpentine.
COURTESAN He did, and from my finger snatched that ring.
ANTIPHOLUS E. 'Tis true, my liege, this ring I had of her.
DUKE Saw'st thou him enter at the abbey here?
COURTESAN As sure, my liege, as I do see your grace.   280
DUKE Why, this is strange. Go call the Abbess hither.
        I think you are all mated, or stark mad.
                                       Exit one to the Abbess
EGEON Most mighty Duke, vouchsafe me speak a word.
        Haply I see a friend will save my life
        And pay the sum that may deliver me.   285
DUKE Speak freely, Syracusian, what thou wilt.
EGEON Is not your name, sir, called Antipholus?
        And is not that your bondman Dromio?
DROMIO E. Within this hour I was his bondman, sir,
        But he, I thank him, gnawed in two my cords.   290
        Now am I Dromio, and his man, unbound.
EGEON I am sure you both of you remember me.
DROMIO E. Ourselves we do remember, sir, by you,
        For lately we were bound as you are now.
        You are not Pinch's patient, are you, sir?   295
EGEON Why look you strange on me? You know me well.
ANTIPHOLUS E. I never saw you in my life till now.

Egeon continues to try to persuade Antipholus of Ephesus and Dromio to recognise him, but is unsuccessful. Egeon suggests his son is ashamed to acknowledge him, but the Duke supports Antipholus' denial.

1 Egeon's appeal to his son

a Change the order (individually, then in pairs)

Write out the four sentences of Egeon's speech (lines 307–18) on four separate pieces of paper. Rearrange the pieces so that the order of the sentences is different from that in the script itself. How many different ways of ordering can you find?

In pairs, discuss which of the alternative orders are interesting. Some will seem to make little sense, but others will suggest something new about the speech. Finally, decide together on one alternative sequence that you will read to the rest of the class. Be prepared to defend your decision!

Then go back to the speech as it appears in the play. Why does it appear in this particular order?

b Asking questions (individually, then in pairs)

Pick out two or three phrases that puzzle you in this same speech (lines 307–18). Then, in pairs, try to solve each other's problem lines. If you are still puzzled, put your problems forward for the class to work on.

c Which phrase do you like best?

Still focusing on the same speech, choose the phrase or line that appeals to you most. Compare notes with others in the class to see if you agree.

---

defeatures disfigurements   **wasting lamps** failing eyesight
extremity extreme cruelty
conduits channels

EGEON O, grief hath changed me since you saw me last,
And careful hours with time's deformèd hand
Have written strange defeatures in my face.   300
But tell me yet, dost thou not know my voice?
ANTIPHOLUS E. Neither.
EGEON Dromio, nor thou?
DROMIO E. No, trust me, sir, nor I.
EGEON   I am sure thou dost.
DROMIO E. Ay, sir, but I am sure I do not, and whatsoever a man   305
denies, you are now bound to believe him.
EGEON Not know my voice? O time's extremity,
Hast thou so cracked and splitted my poor tongue
In seven short years that here my only son
Knows not my feeble key of untuned cares?   310
Though now this grainèd face of mine be hid
In sap-consuming winter's drizzled snow,
And all the conduits of my blood froze up,
Yet hath my night of life some memory,
My wasting lamps some fading glimmer left,   315
My dull deaf ears a little use to hear.
All these old witnesses, I cannot err,
Tell me thou art my son Antipholus.
ANTIPHOLUS E. I never saw my father in my life.
EGEON But seven years since, in Syracusa, boy,   320
Thou know'st we parted. But perhaps, my son,
Thou sham'st to acknowledge me in misery.
ANTIPHOLUS E. The Duke and all that know me in the city
Can witness with me that it is not so.
I ne'er saw Syracusa in my life.   325
DUKE I tell thee, Syracusian, twenty years
Have I been patron to Antipholus,
During which time he ne'er saw Syracusa.
I see thy age and dangers make thee dote.

Aemilia emerges from the abbey with Antipholus of Syracuse and his Dromio. Both sets of twins are on stage. Antipholus of Syracuse recognises his father, and Aemilia recognises her husband, Egeon.

1 Staging the last moments (in pairs, then in large groups)

At the moment Aemilia emerges from the abbey with Antipholus and Dromio of Syracuse (line 330), all the 'errors' of the play begin to be put right and the complications fall away. Everyone realises – though perhaps not all at the same time – that there are two sets of twins, and that Egeon will be reunited with Aemilia and reprieved from his death sentence.

In pairs, plan the positions on stage of the various characters for lines 319–64. In particular, how are you going to arrange the two sets of twins, seen together on stage for the first time? How will they move during the scene?

Then in groups of eleven to fourteen, decide whose plan you are going to try to put into action, and cast the scene. You will need at least:

> Egeon
> Aemilia
> Antipholus of Syracuse
> Antipholus of Ephesus
> Adriana
> Luciana
> Dromio of Syracuse
> Dromio of Ephesus
> Duke
> Angelo
> courtesan

You can add as many attendants or other characters from the play as you wish. Rehearse the scene from line 319 to the end of the play, and then present it to the other half of the class.

---

genius spirit
deciphers tells which is which
at a burden in one birth
rude rough

Enter [AEMILIA,] *the Abbess, with* ANTIPHOLUS OF SYRACUSE *and*
DROMIO OF SYRACUSE

ABBESS Most mighty Duke, behold a man much wronged.   330
                    All gather to see them
ADRIANA I see two husbands, or mine eyes deceive me.
DUKE One of these men is genius to the other;
              And so, of these, which is the natural man,
              And which the spirit? Who deciphers them?
DROMIO S. I, sir, am Dromio. Command him away.   335
DROMIO E. I, sir, am Dromio. Pray let me stay.
ANTIPHOLUS S. Egeon, art thou not? or else his ghost.
DROMIO S. O, my old master! Who hath bound him here?
ABBESS Whoever bound him, I will loose his bonds,
              And gain a husband by his liberty.   340
              Speak, old Egeon, if thou be'st the man
              That hadst a wife once called Æmilia,
              That bore thee at a burden two fair sons.
              O, if thou be'st the same Egeon, speak,
              And speak unto the same Æmilia.   345
DUKE Why, here begins his morning story right.
              These two Antipholus', these two so like,
              And these two Dromios, one in semblance,
              Besides her urging of her wrack at sea –
              These are the parents to these children,   350
              Which accidentally are met together.
EGEON If I dream not, thou art Æmilia.
              If thou art she, tell me, where is that son
              That floated with thee on the fatal raft?
ABBESS By men of Epidamnum he and I   355
              And the twin Dromio all were taken up;
              But by and by rude fishermen of Corinth
              By force took Dromio and my son from them,
              And me they left with those of Epidamnum.
              What then became of them I cannot tell;   360
              I, to this fortune that you see me in.
DUKE [*To Antipholus of Syracuse*] Antipholus, thou cam'st from Corinth
              first.
ANTIPHOLUS S. No, sir, not I. I came from Syracuse.
DUKE Stay, stand apart. I know not which is which.

All is revealed as each character explains the errors made.
The Duke grants Egeon his life without a payment. Aemilia invites
everyone into the abbey to hear each other's stories.

1 Two actors to play the Antipholuses, or one?
(in small groups)

In the 1990 RSC production of the play, both Antipholuses and Dromios were played by one actor each. That is possible up to the previous page, as they are not on stage together. But how can a director get round the problem of having two Antipholuses and two Dromios on stage at the same time? Four characters – two actors!

Talk together about ways in which this could be done.

2 How old are the Antipholuses?
'Thirty-three years have I but gone in travail
Of you, my sons' (line 400)

This makes the two Antipholuses older than you may have thought. Look back at the list of characters in the play, and write down the age you think each one should be. Compare your guesses with others, arguing for your own choices. Lines that might help you decide on their age and on the time-scale of the story are 1.1.125, 1.1.132 and 5.1.309. See also the references on page 60.

---

pawn exchange
my good cheer your good
  company
sympathised jointly shared
travail work, search

ANTIPHOLUS E. I came from Corinth, my most gracious lord.   365
DROMIO E. And I with him.
ANTIPHOLUS E. Brought to this town by that most famous warrior
    Duke Menaphon, your most renownèd uncle.
ADRIANA Which of you two did dine with me today?
ANTIPHOLUS S. I, gentle mistress.
ADRIANA   And are you not my husband?   370
ANTIPHOLUS E. No, I say nay to that.
ANTIPHOLUS S. And so do I. Yet did she call me so,
    And this fair gentlewoman, her sister here,
    Did call me brother. [*To Luciana*] What I told you then
    I hope I shall have leisure to make good,   375
    If this be not a dream I see and hear.
ANGELO That is the chain, sir, which you had of me.
ANTIPHOLUS S. I think it be, sir. I deny it not.
ANTIPHOLUS E. And you, sir, for this chain arrested me.
ANGELO I think I did, sir. I deny it not.   380
ADRIANA [*To Antipholus of Ephesus*] I sent you money, sir, to be your bail
    By Dromio, but I think he brought it not.
DROMIO E. No, none by me.
ANTIPHOLUS S. This purse of ducats I received from you,
    And Dromio my man did bring them me.   385
    I see we still did meet each other's man,
    And I was ta'en for him, and he for me,
    And thereupon these errors are arose.
ANTIPHOLUS E. These ducats pawn I for my father here.
DUKE It shall not need. Thy father hath his life.   390
COURTESAN Sir, I must have that diamond from you.
ANTIPHOLUS E. There, take it, and much thanks for my good cheer.
ABBESS Renownèd Duke, vouchsafe to take the pains
    To go with us into the abbey here,
    And hear at large discoursèd all our fortunes,   395
    And all that are assembled in this place,
    That by this sympathisèd one day's error
    Have suffered wrong. Go, keep us company,
    And we shall make full satisfaction.
    Thirty-three years have I but gone in travail   400
    Of you, my sons, and till this present hour
    My heavy burden ne'er deliverèd.

Aemilia invites everyone to a long overdue baptismal feast. All enter the abbey except the two sets of twins. Dromio of Syracuse mistakes his master's brother for his master. The Dromios leave the stage hand in hand.

1 The most important line?

Which do you think is the most important line on this last page? Compare your choice with others, and be prepared to justify your decision.

2 The 'gossips' feast' (in large groups)

Imagine the characters are sitting around a table, enjoying their reunion and reprieve at the 'gossips' feast'. Shakespeare is there, too. Let general conversation take place, and then begin to focus on particular moments in the play. Questions can be addressed to Shakespeare as well as to each other. You may like to know that Shakespeare had twins (a boy, Hamnet, and a girl, Judith) who would have been about eleven years old at the time of the first performance of the play in 1594.

3 Curtain call (in two large groups)

How would you arrange a curtain call at the end of a performance? Divide the class into two halves. Plan your positions and movements. Show the rest of the class, who will applaud as the audience and also try to identify the characters.

---

gossips' feast a baptismal feast of godparents at which each of the main characters is to be rebaptised

kitchened entertained in the kitchen

draw cuts draw lots (by picking straws)

The Duke, my husband, and my children both,
And you, the calendars of their nativity,
Go to a gossips' feast, and go with me.   405
After so long grief, such nativity.
DUKE With all my heart I'll gossip at this feast.
                    Exeunt omnes, [except] the two Dromios
                        and [the] two brothers [Antipholus]
DROMIO S. [*To Antipholus of Ephesus*] Master, shall I fetch your stuff
     from shipboard?
ANTIPHOLUS E. Dromio, what stuff of mine hast thou embarked?
DROMIO S. Your goods that lay at host, sir, in the Centaur.   410
ANTIPHOLUS S. He speaks to me; I am your master, Dromio.
     Come, go with us, we'll look to that anon.
     Embrace thy brother there, rejoice with him.
                              Exeunt [the brothers Antipholus]
DROMIO S. There is a fat friend at your master's house
     That kitchened me for you today at dinner.   415
     She now shall be my sister, not my wife.
DROMIO E. Methinks you are my glass, and not my brother.
     I see by you I am a sweet-faced youth.
     Will you walk in to see their gossiping?
DROMIO S. Not I, sir. You are my elder.   420
DROMIO E. That's a question. How shall we try it?
DROMIO S. We'll draw cuts for the senior. Till then, lead thou first.
DROMIO E. Nay then, thus:
     We came into the world like brother and brother,
     And now let's go hand in hand, not one before another.   425
                                        Exeunt

Moments from the play

1 Matching illustrations to script

Here are four illustrations from a nineteenth-century edition of *The Comedy of Errors*. In pairs, match the quotations to the illustrations, then find the source of each quotation.

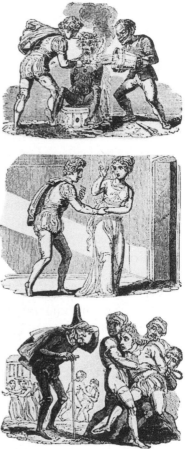

ADR. Back, slave, or I will break thy head across.
DRO. E. And he will bless that cross with other
    beating:
Between you I shall have a holy head.

PINCH. The fiend is strong within him.
LUC. Ah me, poor man, how pale and wan he looks!
ANT. E. What, wilt thou murder me?

SERV. My master and his man are both broke loose,
Beaten the maids a-row, and bound the doctor,
Whose beard they have singed off with brands of fire;
And ever as it blaz'd, they threw on him
Great pails of puddled mire to quench the hair.

ANT. S. Thee will I love, and with thee lead my life;
Thou hast no husband yet, nor I no wife;
Give me thy hand.

2 Framing a moment (in groups of four)

Choose one of the moments above. Prepare a scene – not necessarily connected to the action of *The Comedy of Errors* – in which these lines appear. Your entire scene should last two to five minutes, and include action and dialogue *before* and *after* these lines.

The Comedy of Errors on stage

A first production?

It is thought that *The Comedy of Errors* was first performed on 28 December 1594 at Gray's Inn, London, one of the Inns of Court, the major law schools in England. It was performed as part of a series of revels or entertainments put on by the students or by companies of actors, and took place at one end of a large rectangular hall. Unlike the thrust stage of Shakespeare's Globe on Bankside, the stage in such a hall would have been constructed or improvised to be straight across one end of the hall.

It is possible that for this play the set would have consisted of simple screens or box-like constructions to suggest the three 'houses' that are mentioned in the script. These are: the house of Antipholus and Adriana, recognisable by the sign of the phoenix; the house of the courtesan (an inn, marked by the sign of a 'porpentine' or porcupine); and the priory. The 'mart' or market-place would be centre stage, and roads off to the port would be suggested by spaces between the houses or exits stage right and left.

The Great Hall of Gray's Inn.

Designing your set for the play

Work with a particular space in mind. It could be the drama studio, the school hall, or some other actual location inside (or outside) your school or college. Decide whether your audience will remain seated throughout, or whether you will stage a 'promenade performance' where the audience moves from location to location.

Next, determine the ingredients of your set as suggested by the script of the play. Are you going to have three fixed houses (see page 113), or will you have a more flexible set with the priory only being 'created' for the last scene? Where does the action take place? Think about scene changes. Are changes of scene necessary or can all the action take place on the same set? Remember, the vital thing is for the action to flow smoothly from scene to scene without long delays.

Now make a plan of your space. Show clearly the positions of each item of your set. Label your diagram with comments and quotations from the play. Add any directions you think necessary. You can then:

a sketch your set as seen by the audience
b make a three-dimensional model in card or building blocks
c design signs for the 'houses' (and any other signs you think will help the audience).

If your school or college decides to produce the play, you can become involved in the design and construction of the actual set!

Design the costumes

The general style of the costumes depends on the period in which you want the action of the play to be set. Once you have decided on a *time* and *place* for the action, you can then decide what kind of costumes the Antipholuses, the Dromios, Egeon, the Duke, Adriana and Luciana will wear.

Decide whether you are going to go for a consistent look to the costumes. Many productions try to ensure that all costumes are from the same period and in the same style. But not all do so. If you decide not to be consistent, you need good reasons for your decision.

Costume designs, from the Royal Shakespeare Company (1976) and the
Bristol Old Vic production (1989).

And here are some notes on costume from an 1856 edition of the
play:

Duke	Rich shape with long flowing arm-hole robe of blue velvet, white pantaloons, white shoes, hat and feathers
Egeon	Black velvet dress, arm-hole, cloak, black stockings and shoes
Two Antipholuses	Light blue shapes trimmed with yellow and buttons, blue stockings, russet boots, cross belts, swords, hat and feathers . . .

The language of *The Comedy of Errors*

1 Repetition

Repetition is often used by Shakespeare in *The Comedy of Errors*. One example is in Adriana's first words to Antipholus in 2.2 (lines 104–9):

> The time was once when thou unurged wouldst vow
> That never words were music to thine ear,
> That never object pleasing in thine eye,
> That never touch well welcome to thy hand,
> That never meat sweet-savoured in thy taste,
> Unless I spake, or looked, or touched, or carved to thee.

How many other passages can you find in the play that use repetition in some way? Collect lists, question-and-answer dialogues and other forms. Discuss your findings with others in the class. How many different kinds of repetition can you find? Talk together about reasons for their use.

2 Comic language

The language of the Dromios is full of punning, extended plays on words (conceits) and other kinds of humour. In many ways they are like stand-up comics. Collect your favourite exchanges. Prepare one of these to show to the rest of the class (or record it on tape) What kinds of games with language do the two Dromios play? One example is in the story told by Dromio of Ephesus to Adriana and Luciana of his encounter with Antipholus of Syracuse (2.1.60–64):

> ''Tis dinner-time', quoth I. 'My gold', quoth he.
> 'Your meat doth burn', quoth I. 'My gold', quoth he.
> 'Will you come home?' quoth I. 'My gold', quoth he.
> 'Where is the thousand marks I gave thee, villain?'
> 'The pig', quoth I, 'is burned.' 'My gold', quoth he.

This device of answering something utterly irrelevant to what is asked is called **heterogenium**. Make up an example of your own in the same style.

3 Soliloquies

There are several **soliloquies** in the play. A soliloquy is when one character is alone on stage and talks either to him- or herself, or to the audience. One soliloquy occurs at 1.2.95, when Antipholus of Syracuse reflects on the nature of Ephesus:

> Upon my life, by some device or other
> The villain is o'er-raught of all my money.
> They say this town is full of cozenage,
> As nimble jugglers that deceive the eye,
> Dark-working sorcerers that change the mind,
> Soul-killing witches that deform the body . . .

Identify the other soliloquies in the play. All are quite short, so you can write them out. When you think you have found every one, compare your collection with other groups in the class. What differences can you find between the language of the soliloquies and that of the rest of the play? Work on one of the soliloquies to deliver to *your* audience.

4 Imagery

One example of imagery in the play is in Antipholus' lines 'I to the world am like a drop of water that in the ocean seeks another drop' (1.2.35–6). It can be linked to the presence of the sea in the play and to the theme of identity. Another example is the network of images that cluster around the chain (or necklace) that Angelo has made for Antipholus of Ephesus, the chains that bind Egeon, and the prison shackles that Antipholus and Dromio of Ephesus are bound by in Act 4.

Sometimes the imagery runs like a thread through the woven material of the play. At other times a single image has a dramatic as well as textual function, as in Adriana's 'Thou art an elm, my husband, I a vine' and the lines following (2.2.165–71), which were all triggered by the word 'fasten' in line 164.

Make a list of some of the images from *The Comedy of Errors*, and then identify what you take to be the most important imagery in the play.

What is *The Comedy of Errors* about?

As in all Shakespeare plays, there's no simple, single answer to the question 'What's this play about?'. Here are a few suggestions to help your thinking.

1 Themes

Put the following statements in order of priority. Discuss the relative importance of each.

The Comedy of Errors is about:

- the nature of marriage
- the obligations of women in marriage
- a quest for identity by a main character
- the nature of jealousy
- twins and their problems
- madness and how to cure it
- the importance of family life
- making mistakes
- how people are misled by appearances
- servants and masters.

You might want to add further statements, or to change the wording of some of these statements.

Take the statement you believe to be the most important. Make a list of moments and incidents in the play which support your view of the importance of this theme. Collect quotations to illustrate this theme. The following is an example on the theme of madness.

Madness and how to cure it

- Antipholus of Syracuse and his Dromio seem to think they are in 'fairyland', where everything seems topsy-turvy and magical. e.g.

> 'Wast thou mad
> That thus so madly thou didst answer me?' (2.2.11–12)

and, after the urging of Adriana to take dinner with her:

> 'Am I in earth, in heaven, or in hell?
> Sleeping or waking? mad or well advised?' (2.2.203-4)

- In Act 4, Scene 4, Dr Pinch is called in to exorcise the 'madness' that seems to have taken over Antipholus and Dromio of Ephesus. Pinch declares:

  'Mistress, both man and master is possessed;
  I know it by their pale and deadly looks.
  They must be bound and laid in some dark room'. (4.4.86–8ff)

- In the last act, the Duke thinks:

  'you are all mated, or stark mad'. (5.1.282)

This is just a beginning – there are many more references to madness, its treatment and cure.

Use this raw material as the basis for an essay on the play. Frame a question you will try to answer, e.g. 'What is the most important theme in *The Comedy of Errors?*' or 'How is the theme of madness developed in *The Comedy of Errors?*'. As an alternative, you could hold a debate to argue the relative importance of the various themes in the play.

2 Is the first scene really necessary?

Some people believe that Shakespeare always tells you the theme of the play in the first scene or even in the first few lines. The first scene of *The Comedy of Errors* seems to promise a tragedy rather than a comedy. Would it be possible to cut it, and begin the play with 'Therefore give out you are of Epidamnum' at Act 2, Scene 1? What would be lost? Argue the case either for the inclusion or exclusion of this scene.

3 Who are the most important characters?

Look at the list of characters on page 1. Rearrange it in two ways. First, in order of the importance of the characters in the play from your point of view. Where do the women come in your list? Second, in a way that makes it clear to the audience how the characters are linked with each other.

4 St Paul's 'Letter to the Ephesians'

Read St Paul's 'Letter to the Ephesians' in the New Testament. What connections can you discover between this and *The Comedy of Errors?*

Twins

Twins have always fascinated scientists. In the 1980s a study of twins took place in America at the University of Minnesota. Peter Watson has published a book *Twins* based on this study. Like the characters in *The Comedy of Errors*, the sets of twins in the study were separated from just after birth and raised in different households, often in different countries. One case study was of a pair of twins brought together after a period of forty-six years. Separated at six months, one was brought up a Jew in Trinidad, the other a member of Hitler Youth in Germany. At their first meeting they discovered:

both wore identical rectangular wire-rimmed spectacles with rounded corners
both read magazines back to front
both wore blue shirts with breast pockets and epaulettes
both absent-mindedly stored rubber bands on their wrists
both liked reading in restaurants
both had recurrent anxiety and explosive anger fits
both enjoyed the joke of sneezing loudly to watch the reactions of others.

1 A study of twins

Make your own study of twins. Base your research on either the study of an actual pair of twins you know, or by researching in books.

2 Autobiography of a twin

If you are a twin, you might like to write an autobiographical piece. If not, can you imagine what it is like to be a twin? Write a fictional autobiography.

3 An essay on the twins

Write a comparison of the twin brothers and servants in *The Comedy of Errors*. Concentrate on their similarities and differences.

4 A long lost twin

Someone who is a mirror-image of yourself walks into the room. What happens?

George Vining and J. Nelson as the two Antipholuses, Princess's Theatre, 1864.

5 Hamnet and Judith Shakespeare

Shakespeare's own twins were born in 1585. Hamnet died in 1596, Judith in 1662. Imagine Judith's thoughts on *The Comedy of Errors*.

6 Twins in Twelfth Night

In Shakespeare's *Twelfth Night*, the sister and brother twins, Viola and Sebastian, are central to the plot. Find out how they are like and unlike the Antipholuses in *The Comedy of Errors*. Focus on their characters and on their actions in the plays. Present your findings in the form of an essay or a television interview of the characters. A meeting between the sets of twins from different plays could be very fruitful!

Make your own programme for
The Comedy of Errors

Some contents of a theatre programme:

- a summary of the plot
- source material stories and other material that Shakespeare might have used for inspiration
- documentary material illustrating the themes of the play, e.g. twins, marriage, shipwreck, madness
- literary material (e.g. poems by Shakespeare or others which illuminate the play)
- a cast list
- pen portraits or biographies of the actors
- rehearsal photographs
- critical viewpoints (quotations from essays on the play)
- statements by the director and actors
- quotations from the play
- maps
- a stage history and illustrations of past productions
- advertisements

You have crucial decisions to make about your own programme:

a What size will it be?
b What kind of paper will you use?
c What kind of binding – will you staple, sew or simply fold it?
d What kind of print – handwritten, typed or word-processed?
e How many pages?
f What will be the contents of each page?
g Will each person in the group work on a particular aspect of the programme? Who does what?
h How will the programme be printed?
i How many should be printed?
j Over what time period will you be working?
k What cover illustration will you use?
l What will it cost? What price will you charge?

Opposite is an example of an illustration from a Rumanian production in 1964–5.

See a version of *The Comedy of Errors*

You may be able to visit a production of *The Comedy of Errors*. How can you find out if there is a production currently running or about to open? Prepare for and follow up a visit through one or more of the following:

- Everyone chooses a character (or an incident or scene) to watch especially closely. Write down your expectations before you go. Report back to the class on how your expectations for *your* character or scene were fulfilled or challenged.
- Compare the production to others you have seen or to film or video versions. Were any scenes omitted or shortened? What was the setting? Was anything added to the script?
- Write your own review. Be specific about different aspects of the production: casting, the delivery of lines, costumes and pace. Your review should record your own perceptions of what you actually saw and heard – and your feelings about the production.

Most importantly, enjoy it!

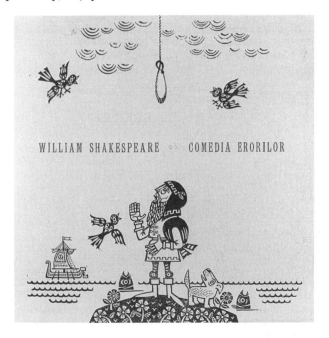

William Shakespeare 1564–1616

1564 Born Stratford-upon-Avon, eldest son of John and Mary Shakespeare.
1582 Married to Anne Hathaway of Shottery, near Stratford.
1583 Daughter, Susanna, born.
1585 Twins, son and daughter, Hamnet and Judith, born.
1592 First mention of Shakespeare in London. Robert Greene, another playwright, described Shakespeare as 'an upstart crow beautified with our feathers . . .'. Greene seems to have been jealous of Shakespeare. He mocked Shakespeare's name, calling him 'the only Shake-scene in a country' (presumably because Shakespeare was writing successful plays).
1595 A shareholder in 'The Lord Chamberlain's Men', an acting company that became extremely popular.
1596 Son Hamnet died, aged eleven.
Father, John, granted arms (acknowledged as a gentleman).
1597 Bought New Place, the grandest house in Stratford.
1598 Acted in Ben Jonson's *Every Man in His Humour*.
1599 Globe Theatre opens on Bankside. Performances in the open air.
1601 Father, John, dies.
1603 James I granted Shakespeare's company a royal patent: 'The Lord Chamberlain's Men' became 'The King's Men' and played about twelve performances each year at court.
1607 Daughter, Susanna, marries Dr John Hall.
1608 Mother, Mary, dies.
1609 'The King's Men' begin performing indoors at Blackfriars Theatre.
1610 Probably returned from London to live in Stratford.
1616 Daughter, Judith, marries Thomas Quiney.
Died. Buried in Holy Trinity Church, Stratford-upon-Avon.

The plays and poems
(no one knows exactly when he wrote each play)

1589–1595 *The Two Gentlemen of Verona, The Taming of the Shrew, First, Second and Third Parts of King Henry VI, Titus Andronicus, King Richard III, The Comedy of Errors, Love's Labour's Lost, A Midsummer Night's Dream, Romeo and Juliet, King Richard II* (and the long poems *Venus and Adonis* and *The Rape of Lucrece*).

1596–1599 *King John, The Merchant of Venice, First and Second Parts of King Henry IV, The Merry Wives of Windsor, Much Ado About Nothing, King Henry V, Julius Caesar* (and probably the *Sonnets*).

1600–1605 *As You Like It, Hamlet, Twelfth Night, Troilus and Cressida, Measure for Measure, Othello, All's Well That Ends Well, Timon of Athens, King Lear.*

1606–1611 *Macbeth, Antony and Cleopatra, Pericles, Coriolanus, The Winter's Tale, Cymbeline, The Tempest.*

1613 *King Henry VIII, The Two Noble Kinsmen* (both probably with John Fletcher)

1623 Shakespeare's plays published as a collection (now called the First Folio).